KARATE: BEGINNER TO b
IS AN INNOVATIVE INSTRU   ιεXT
ESPECIALLY DESIGNED FOR YOUNG
PEOPLE.

BECAUSE IT IS INTENDED PRIMARILY FOR
HOME STUDY AND SELF-TEACHING, THERE
IS STRONG EMPHASIS ON SAFETY AND
HEALTH.

THE SUBJECT MATTER COVERS A WIDE
RANGE, INCLUDING ROUTINES WHICH CAN
BE PRACTICED ALONE (KATA FORMS),
ROUTINES WHICH CAN BE PRACTICED WITH
A PARTNER (WAZA FORMS), AND A GUIDE
TO FREE-STYLE SPARRING (KUMITE).

USING THE TRADITIONAL MATERIAL
FROM SEVERAL STYLES OF KARATE,
BRUCE TEGNER HAS SELECTED TECHNIQUES
AND DEVISED PROCEDURES WHICH ARE
CONSISTENT WITH MODERN CONCEPTS OF
PHYSICAL EDUCATION AND A HUMANISTIC
APPROACH TO SPORT.

KARATE

BEGINNER TO BLACK BELT

BRUCE TEGNER

THOR PUBLISHING COMPANY   VENTURA   CA   93002

Library of Congress Cataloging in Publication Data

Tegner, Bruce.
    Karate, beginner to black belt.

    Includes index.
    Summary: An introduction to karate techniques from
basic to advanced, emphasizing safety, health, and fitness.
    1. Karate. [1. Karate] I. Title.

GV1114.3.T423   796.8'153   81-18199

ISBN 0-87407-040-6 (pbk.)

Manuscript prepared under the supervision of
ALICE McGRATH

KARATE: Beginner to Black Belt

THOR PUBLISHING COMPANY
P.O. BOX 1782
VENTURA, CA 93002   *Printed in U.S.A.*

BRUCE TEGNER BOOKS REVIEWED

KARATE: BEGINNER to BLACK BELT
"Techniques and routines...illustrated in profuse detail...a fine introduction and a worthwhile reference source...specially geared to a YA audience." KLIATT YOUNG ADULT PB BOOK GUIDE

SELF-DEFENSE: A BASIC COURSE
"An eminently practical, concise guide to self-defense...for young men..." American Library Association BOOKLIST

"YA - A calm, nonsexist approach to simple yet effective self-defense techniques...clear photographs...sound advice." SCHOOL LIBRARY JOURNAL

BRUCE TEGNER'S COMPLETE BOOK OF JUJITSU
"...authoritative and easy-to-follow text..." SCHOOL LIBRARY JOURNAL

BRUCE TEGNER'S COMPLETE BOOK OF SELF-DEFENSE
Recommended for Y.A. in the American Library Association BOOKLIST

SELF-DEFENSE & ASSAULT PREVENTION FOR GIRLS & WOMEN (with Alice McGrath)
"...should be required reading for all girls and women..." WILSON LIBRARY BULLETIN

"...simple and straightforward with no condescension...easy to learn and viable as defense tactics..." SCHOOL LIBRARY JOURNAL

SELF-DEFENSE FOR YOUR CHILD (with Alice McGrath)
[For elementary school-age boys & girls]
"...informative, readable book for family use..." CHRISTIAN HOME & SCHOOL

DEFENSE TACTICS FOR LAW ENFORCEMENT
"...a practical tool for police academy programs, police programs at the university level, and for the (individual) officer..." THE POLICE CHIEF

KUNG FU & TAI CHI: Chinese Karate and Classical Exercise
"...recommended for physical fitness collections." LIBRARY JOURNAL

SOLO FORMS of Karate, Tai Chi, Aikido & Kung Fu (with Alice McGrath)
"...well-coordinated, step-by-step instructions...carefully captioned photos...for personal enjoyment and exercise..." YA American Library Association BOOKLIST

STICK-FIGHTING: SPORT FORMS
"...illustrations and directions are clear and easy to follow... based on foil fencing, quarterstaff and broadsword...in addition to sports-oriented use...might prove of value to drama students..." American Library Association BOOKLIST

CONTENTS

Techniques are demonstrated in the photos by the author and

RICHARD WINDISHAR

DANIEL SCHNEIDER

EDWARD GIBBS

RICHARD GENTRY

and

Keane Murikami

Jim Knutson

INTRODUCTION

MARTIAL ARTS

The term "martial arts" is widely used today to designate forms of hand-to-hand fighting which developed in Asian countries. I use the term because of its general acceptance, but it is a convenience, not a definition. It includes too much and not enough.

All the martial arts have their origins in combat skills, but among them today there is such a wide range of objectives, concepts, procedures and techniques that putting them into one category is confusing.

Some specialties of the martial arts are practiced for recreation and fitness, some for self-defense, and others are tournament sports. Today's adaptations of the martial arts include the lovely, gentle movements of tai chi, the heavy power punching of some styles of karate, formalized *sumo* wrestling, the stylized routines of aikido, practical self-defense based on jujitsu, and sport judo as it is played in the Olympic Games.

The Zen Buddhist influence is important in some of the martial arts. Others are concerned only with fighting skill or fitness exercises. Concepts range from glorification of feudal attitudes (identifying with samurai warriors) to an appreciation of the health and safety concerns of modern physical education.

If "martial arts" included boxing and Western styles of archery and fencing, it would be more accurate. These and other Western sports also derive from ancient battle skills and have been modified for present-day recreation and competition.

Though there are literally hundreds of styles of fighting and many more hundreds of substyles, all fighting methods can be classified according to their use of a fairly small group of basic techniques. They are: weaponless hand and foot blows, throwing and tripping techniques, immobilization and twisting of the joints, the use of "found" weapons such as sticks or stones, or the use of crafted weapons. Some of the martial arts use a small number of techniques from a single category and some use techniques from several or all of the categories, combining the material in various ways to produce the various specialties.

KARATE

Karate is the generic term for many styles of the martial arts which use hand and foot blows as their primary techniques. It is thought that a form of karate originated in Tibet, was introduced to China, and from there spread to the other Asian countries. In each country adaptations occurred and stylistic differences developed.

Kung fu, or gung fu, wu shu and pa kua are among the Chinese styles of karate. Tai kwan do and hapkido are Korean styles. Okinawa-te is practiced in Okinawa. Tai boxing, or Siamese boxing, is another style, and is thought to have influenced savate, French fist-and-foot fighting.

But no matter what name is used, the many styles of karate have this in common: they all use a relatively small group of hand blows and kicking techniques. An open hand slashing blow is, after all, an open hand slashing blow whether it is used in kenpo karate, shito-ryu, or called by a Japanese, Korean, Chinese or English name.

STYLES

Some karate styles emphasize hand blows more than kicking techniques. Some styles emphasize foot blows. Some styles train to develop power and strength (the hard schools), while others train for speed and precision (the soft schools).

Some of the differences are more subtle. Watching several styles of karate being practiced, an intelligent novice might have difficulty discerning the stylistic characteristics. For example, one style of karate might favor certain stances or a particular hand or foot position while using exactly the same hand and foot blows as another style which favors a different beginning stance or foot position. Such stylistic variations are usually a matter of personal preference and have little bearing on karate as practiced by most people.

The history of karate and other specialties of the martial arts has been one of dissident groups breaking off from established centers. The dissidents establish their own school or system from which other groups eventually splinter to establish yet another style. Each group which breaks from the parent school justifies its own existence and its right to separate and criticizes the group which may later separate from it. The passionate adherents of each system, the true believers of a particular school, are the heretics, radicals and scandalizers of the schools from which they have emerged.

A slight stylistic difference is shown here in the foot positions.

BEST STYLE?

Today there are about a dozen main styles of karate, with many substyles and hundreds of sub-substyles. Each teacher believes that his style is best. If there is, in fact, a "best" style, we must ask why there is no consensus and why there are still so many variations in karate styles. The answer suggests itself: There is no "best" karate. There are personal preferences for different schools, teachers, and styles.

In karate competition, players from different schools, using different styles of play, have shown that no single style of play predominates among contest winners. As in any other sport, the champions generally have a highly individual style and an extremely high level of skill. In formal karate, where the performance of routines is the favored method of practice, personal preference is the only gauge by which to evaluate and select a style.

The more one examines the question of comparing styles of karate to evaluate the advantages of one style against another, the more clear it becomes that no objective test is possible. I have heard it seriously proposed that the way to determine which is the best style of karate would be to match players in a fight to the death. The only thing such a match would prove would be the recklessness and foolishness of the promoters and combatants. It is a waste of time and energy to argue the question of "best" karate. There are only styles which suit different people in different circumstances and different situations.

BELT DEGREES

In their original forms, when they were used for hand-to-hand combat, there were no colored belt degrees to rank proficiency in the martial arts. The proficiency of the fighter was determined by his ability to survive. Like archery and sword-fighting, the ancient specialties of weaponless combat have become obsolete for battle. And like archery and fencing, karate has been modified for sport play.

The first of the martial arts to rank proficiency by awarding colored belts was judo. At the end of the last century, Dr. Jigaro Kano, the founder of judo, introduced the practice of ranking skill in judo. Beginning students wore a white belt with the judo uniform, intermediate skill was indicated by a brown belt, and the highly skilled judo player was allowed to wear a black belt. The gradations of skill between beginner and black belt were not marked by different colored belts, but were designated within the rank. For instance, within the brown belt rank there were three degrees of proficiency.

Karate players adopted the general pattern of colored belt ranking, using the white, brown and black belt ranks. As the martial arts became popular throughout the world, schools in different countries adopted their own systems of ranking and used different progressions of colored belts to designate skill level.

In some schools and styles of karate, belt degrees are awarded solely for performance of kata routines and in these systems the kata performance is regarded as the "purest" style of karate. Other schools and systems award belt degrees solely on contest ability. In such systems, the winners of contest matches are promoted to a higher rank.

Still other systems award belt ranking for performance of kata and waza routines, or a combination of performance of formal routines and contest ability. In some systems of karate, belt ranks are awarded solely at the discretion of the head teacher.

No system of school recognizes the belt ranking of other systems and schools. There is no generally accepted, standard belt-ranking system. Therefore, a belt rank has no significance outside of the school in which it was awarded. Belt ranks indicate not only a different type of achievement in different systems, but a different level of skill. It is not possible to compare belt rankings of karate players in different systems. Their *skill* might be evaluated in a contest, but not by the color of belt or designation of rank. In one style of karate a particular stage of training might be indicated by awarding a green belt and a comparable level of skill might be designated by a purple belt in a different system.

There is one inflexible rule in the martial arts, as there is in most areas where proficiency is evaluated and graded in some way: Under no circumstances is it possible to award yourself a rating. Even if you have conscientiously and seriously practiced all the techniques in any of the rank sections, you may not call yourself a purple, brown, or black belt holder, just as you may not award yourself a high school diploma or give yourself a driver's license.

THIS SYSTEM

Over the years I have developed the system of karate which is presented to you in this book. It is a system based on several styles of karate. I have selected the techniques and arranged the material in what I believe to be the most useful for individuals studying alone and have divided it into sections that are characteristic of proficiency ranking found in many styles of karate.

Because players may not award belt ranks to themselves and many of you may not have access to a school or club, I would suggest that you form your own club with a physical education instructor or a youth group leader as your sponsor. Belt ranks could be awarded in such a club, using standards agreed upon by the group with the clear understanding that the belt degrees would have significance solely within the group.

Because of the selection and organization of the karate material in this book, any person who is experienced in teaching physical activities can use this text to supervise group practice--unison solo forms, two-man forms, and sparring. With a physical education background, the teacher does not need formal karate training to supervise karate practice as it is presented here. The adaptations to modern use, the safety precautions and the style of the work were all designed for the use of those who do not have access to professional instruction and for the use of physical education instructors whose background does not include martial arts training.

KUNG FU/KARATE IN MOVIES & T.V.

Kung fu and other styles of karate and other martial arts have been widely publicized and exploited in films and on television.

While these show fights have stimulated great interest in the subject field, they have also fostered fantasies and distorted the reality of ancient and modern applications of karate. Some have romanticized and glorified warrior training for personal vengeance.

Filmed fight scenes are meant to convince us, while we are looking at them, that they are true, even when our intelligence tells us that they are film scenes in which actors win when the script calls for them to win and lose when the script is written for them to lose.

After each fight scene is carefully written for the maximum thrill, every fight scene is carefully designed, choreographed, rehearsed and photographed for maximum action effect. Every frame of every filmed fight scene you see has been planned in advance, shot from special angles, and edited to remove any missteps in the action. Trampolines are used to send the heroes and villains flying into the fray. Sound effects are added to enhance the illusion of contact.

If fight scenes were in reality what they appear to be on the screen, there would be nobody left to report for the second day of filming. But the actors and the stunt men get up after a series of "deadly" karate fights and do it over again for as long as it takes to get the perfect scene on film.

The "winner" of a movie fight does not win because of a superior method of fighting or because of superior fighting skill. The story and the script determine who wins and who loses.

Although there are karate-trained people in some television shows and in some of the movies, the real ability of the individual acting the role of karate fighter is not indicated by what happens on the screen. It has been my experience as a participant in many film projects that the stunt men who "lose" fights are often much better fighters (in real life) than the heroes who "win" fights because that is the way the script reads. In fact, I have choreographed fight scenes, working out every small detail of it in advance, and then trained the hero to "win" the fight and then, in the same film, portrayed the villain, "losing" the fight to the man I trained to "win" it. A good stunt man is one who makes the hero look good by "losing" with as much realism as his acting ability allows.

The movies are not meant to give us instruction; they are meant to give us entertainment. Enjoy them while you are watching them, but don't let the films confuse you about what is make-believe and what is real.

HAND CONDITIONING

Spectacular "super-human" breaking tricks are a common feature of film and television exploitation karate. The "secrets" of karate, which account for the ability to perform heavy board- and brick-breaking, are: intensive long-term practice and extreme hand conditioning.

Hand conditioning is a deliberate process of toughening, desensitizing and callousing the hands, so that they can be used as "weapons." The conditioning is achieved by striking hard surfaces repeatedly until injury occurs. As the injury heals, scar tissue forms. Eventually, the hands become toughened, insensitive, and impervious to pain. When this happens, knuckle blows of full force can be directed against hard surfaces.

Extreme hand conditioning may injure the hands and impair ability to perform skills which require manual dexterity and sensitivity. Because young people are the major group presently interested in karate, I cannot stress too much the negative aspect of hand conditioning. Hand conditioning, which you might do just for fun when you are young, could have an effect on your life as an adult--preventing you from acquiring valuable job skills and limiting your job opportunities.

When karate was used as unarmed combat against a sword-armed enemy and when the bare hands of the karate fighter had to break through wooden armor, hand conditioning was a necessary procedure. For the modern student of karate, hand conditioning is less than useless; it is harmful, it is ugly and it is irreversible.

KARATE & SELF-DEFENSE

In my earlier karate books, I included sections on special aspects of karate that could be used for self-defense. Since those earlier books were written, I have more fully developed practical techniques of self-defense which are related to karate and jujitsu, but which have been considerably modified to meet the needs of real people in the real world. These books are clearly identified as texts for practical self-defense. In them I have presented general and special self-defense courses, among them a course of defense tactics for law enforcement.

Therefore, this book deals solely with the recreation, fitness, health and sport aspects of karate for today.*

KATA, WAZA & KUMITE

The four principal methods of practicing karate techniques are: single techniques from a standstill, kata forms, waza routines, and free-style kumite.

In most schools and styles of karate, the students spend a great deal of time practicing a single technique from a standstill. After they have perfected the techniques from a standstill, with many repetitions, they advance to the practice of kata forms.

The katas--solo forms--are prearranged series of movements-- hand and foot blows, and parries and blocks--performed in a manner which simulate attack and defense tactics as though against a moving opponent or opponents.

It is my view, based on experience, that students who are practicing karate for fitness and recreation make good progress and enjoy the activity more if they begin to practice katas (and wazas) when they have achieved basic skill in the performance of the separate hand and foot blows and modes of moving. It is in the practice of the routines that they strive to perfect technical skill.

The organization of this book is based on the premise that the student will spend relatively little time in learning the material which precedes the training katas, and will devote as much time as necessary, and available, in practice of the more interesting material.

*A descriptive listing of self-defense books is available from Thor Publishing Company, P.O. Box 1782, Ventura, CA 93002.

Begin the practice of the katas with attention to gesture and movement. The pace should be relatively slow at the beginning. As skill develops with practice, you can speed up the fast movements and reduce the speed of the slow movements. There are several slow movements in the second purple belt kata, but alternate fast and slow movements do not occur until you reach the second kata of the third brown belt series.

The black belt series of katas are performed in very slow motion and are exceptionally handsome when performed with skill and control.

The wazas--two-man forms--are prearranged routines for two people. Partners take turns performing the attack and defense roles. Preceding the first waza in the purple belt series there is an explanation of safety procedures and the method and style of practicing and demonstrating the waza series.

Kumite (pronounced koo-mee-tay, with equal stress on the three syllables) is free-style sparring. Kumite can be practiced for exercise only or it can be practiced in preparation for contest or tournament--sport karate. For a group practicing without a professional or skilled leader or teacher, I recommend sparring practice using *only* the low-risk-of-injury point-winning target areas. The low-risk/high-risk areas are explained in the section on sparring which follows the black belt kata series.

MEMORIZING THE KATAS

A major benefit to be gained from practicing the katas is the mental stimulation/relaxation resulting from learning the sequence of movements in the katas.

Mental stimulation derives from thinking about the movements and memorizing the patterns. Relaxation is gained through concentration on the kata, diverting your thoughts from the worrisome daily preoccupations and frustrations of life and fixing them on a fresh and absorbing mental/ physical activity.

There are two distinct ways of memorizing a long sequence of movements. Choose the one which suits your situation and your temperament.

THE SHORT-GROUP METHOD

This method is excellent for those whose practice time at
any one session is limited and for those who are engaging
in solo practice without a partner. Because a person
practicing alone must refer to the book at frequent inter-
vals to learn the movements the short-group method is
appropriate.

As the name implies, the short-group method involves
taking small parts of each routine, from four to six movements, and practicing that small portion over and over. When
that small sequence is learned, you proceed to learn the next
few movements and practice those intensively.

When you have practiced five or six short groups, you then
assemble them into one longer sequence. Then you begin
the next short groups. When you have learned the next
five or six groups, assemble them into one sequence and then
join the two longer sequences into one.

Proceed in this manner until you have learned all the movements of a routine and can perform them in a single, unin-
terrupted sequence.

THE LONG-GROUP METHOD

If you have a practice partner who can read the movements
aloud as you perform them, or if you find this method more
to your liking, follow this procedure: practice the maximum
number of movements of a routine which you can cover in
a single session.

When the long-group method is used, progress in memori-
zation does not appear to be as rapid as when the short-
group method is used, but for many individuals, the long-
group method is suitable. If you are not sure which of the
two methods is better for you, try them both and select
the one which gives you the best results.

Specialists in the psychology of learning and memory
believe that the long-group method of memorizing results
in longer retention of the learned material. Using the
long-group method, you will not memorize the movements
in sequence as quickly as in the short-group method, but it
is likely that you will remember them better and for a
longer time once you do memorize them.

If you do not have a practice partner, you might find someone who would be willing to read the movements aloud to you so that you can practice without constant references to the book, though you should study the photos carefully before you begin so that you will have a clear mental image of the gesture of each movement.

KI-AI

Ki-ai, also called ki-ya or ki-yai, is the conscious use of an energy concentration technique which most of us use unconsciously from time to time.

When you have a heavy job to do--lifting, pulling or pushing--you are likely to follow a pattern of behavior, without thinking about it, to prepare for and produce a surge of power. You take a deep breath and then grunt as you complete the action.

Most of us have great stores of potential energy and mental capability which we do not use. There are many ways of releasing the potential powers we store. Fear, determination, religious beliefs, shock, crisis situations, anger and insanity are possible triggers to set off the physiological and psychological impulses that expand the limits of normal ability.

A small woman lifts a tremendous weight to save her child. A man stays awake an incredible length of time to avoid death in a crisis situation. An individual sustains a serious injury which he does not experience as painful until long after it has occurred. In a hypnotic state, someone demonstrates a degree of physical control not thought possible under normal conditions.

Some of the limits we set for mental and physical effort are self-protecting. We could not constantly subject our bodies to surge-power effort without ill effects. We need to feel pain, strain and fatigue to some degree or we would be in constant peril of life-threatening or health-threatening overexertion.

Between the extreme of overexertion and the extreme of underutilization of power, there is the conscious development of natural potential through concentration and focus. And even though the power that is developed in the practice of karate katas and wazas is not exerted as force with impact, it is real. You can see the difference between a punch or kick that is delivered with surge power and one that is not; you can feel the difference when you deliver a technique with full focus and concentration.

Ki-ai is the technique of using the unconscious inhale-and-grunt behavior for conscious focus and concentration.

There are two distinct phases of ki-ai: the windup and the thrust. The first phase prepares; the second phase delivers.

In the windup phase, concentrate. Take a deep breath, tighten your abdominal muscles and focus your attention on the specific action to come. In the thrust phase, exhale sharply as you deliver the hand or foot blow.

Ki-ai can be silent (except for the sound of breath being forcefully expelled) or sounded. When it is sounded, any number of different sounds can be used. *Ai* and *hai* are commonly used, but many karate and judo players shout *zut* or *huh*, or they hiss as they exhale and effect the critical action.

In the performance of the katas, breathe fully and regularly throughout most of the routine and use silent ki-ai to add dramatic weight to any of the movements you want to emphasize.

The wazas can be performed with sounded ki-ai each time the countermove occurs in the routine. Or you can practice the wazas with silent ki-ai if you prefer.

In sparring practice and in contest, sounded ki-ai is often used when attempting a point-scoring technique, but not throughout the match. Karate exploitation films exaggerate the extent to which sounded ki-ai is used; the shouting is recorded on a sound track made at a different time than when the fight is filmed. If they actually shouted as much as they seem to in the films, the combatants would be exhausted from shouting before they could spring off the trampolines to scatter their multiple opponents.

BELT DEGREE REQUIREMENTS

Remembering always that belt degrees awarded in one club or school are only significant in that school or system, the independent club or school can use the following guide for ranking skill. Because the requirements have been developed for independent studies and for physical education and recreation, they do not include winning contest points as a condition for promotion. The sparring requirement is fulfilled by demonstrating the ability to use karate hand and foot blows, and blocks, parries, feints and counters without prearrangment. At the higher belt levels it is fulfilled by demonstrating skill in the application of strategy and tactics to free-style play.

White Belt: All students are designated "white belt" when they begin. When they are familiar with the material through page 41, and can perform the training katas, the teacher or leader assigns "advanced white belt" status and they proceed to learn and practice the purple belt katas and wazas.

Performance of the katas and wazas is judged by the teacher or leader, or by a club committee. The standard of performance should be the same for all students.

Purple Belt: For advancement to the rank of purple belt the candidates should demonstrate competence in the performance of the purple belt katas and wazas and demonstrate the ability to spar in give-and-take form.

Third Brown Belt: For promotion to third brown belt, the katas and wazas should be demonstrated with very good form and candidates should have the ability to spar free-style.

Second Brown Belt: The second brown belt waza series should be demonstrated with excellent technique and candidates should demonstrate a high level of competence in free-style sparring.

First Brown Belt: The ninety-movement form should be done with near-perfection of technique. Sparring ability should be highly developed.

Black Belt: For promotion to black belt level, candidates must perform the slow-movement katas to perfection and demonstrate free-style sparring with expert skill.

Although they are not yet accepted in open tournament, where other safety measures may be taken, students practicing from this book should use ONLY the low-risk target areas for sparring.

SLIDE-STEP

Many of the movements in the routines include a sliding
step, a move made without lifting your foot from the floor.
The slide-step can be done flat-footed, or slightly onto the
ball of the foot. For sparring, the slide-step lets you move
easily and quickly without loss of balance.

PIVOTS

Pivoting is another way to move lightly and gracefully.
To pivot on your right foot, shift your weight onto the ball
of the foot and turn it without lifting your foot from the
floor. You can step with your left foot, or slide-step. Your
body will shift to follow the pivot.

Do not pivot flat-footed.

To pivot on both feet, rise slightly onto the balls of both
feet and turn without lifting either foot from the floor.

Practice the pivots a few times before beginning work on
the katas and wazas. Alternate practice of right and left
foot pivots and pivot on both feet. Practice turning in all
directions. Pivot quarter turns, half turns and full turns.
As you use and practice the pivots in the routines, you will
develop the ability to use pivots to achieve efficiency in
movement.

DIRECTIONS

The directions in the text are given as fixed compass points.
At first, you may find it useful to place markers on the
floor to indicate the four points--north, south, east and west.

*The text is numerically keyed to the photographs. Where
there is no photograph, you will find the symbol "†" and
where you are referred to a photo previously shown, you
will also find the symbol "†."*

STANCES & GUARDS

Stances and guards are used as beginning positions for the
katas and wazas and they have tactical applications in
karate sparring and contest.

The stance and the two guards which occur most often
in the following katas and wazas are shown here. Other
stances and guards will be shown and explained where they
occur.

HORSE STANCE

1. This is a strong stance taken with the feet apart, knees bent and the upper body erect. Commonly, the horse stance is taken with palms-up fists held at the sides of the body.

2. The term "horse stance" is thought to derive from "horse-riding stance" and in the side view the horse-riding position is seen more clearly.

GUARDS

3. The low fist guard is taken with a wide "T" foot position for good balance. One fist is drawn back. The arm of the leading fist is fully extended.

4. The high fist guard differs only with respect to the leading fist position--it is raised.

       5   6   7

PUNCHING

The striking point of the karate punch is the area of the two large knuckles. At the conclusion of the action, the punching arm is fully extended.

Practice delivering one-two punches from the horse stance.

5. Assume the horse stance with your fists at your sides, palms up.

6. As you take a short step forward with your right foot, turn your right fist over as you punch straight out, wheeling your upper body slightly to add body power to the blow. Hesitate briefly.

7. As you step forward with your left foot, punch forward with your left fist, turning it over as you punch, and snap your right fist back to your side.

Practice punching from a guard stance.

8. From a low fist guard, leading with your left fist and left foot and with your right fist at your side . . .

9. . . . step with your right foot as you start to reverse hand positions . . .

10. . . . punching forward with your right fist as you snap your left fist to your side.

8   9   10

SLASH BLOW

11. To deliver the slash blow, your hand
is held slightly cupped and firm, but not
rigid. Your thumb is close to or along-
side your index finger. The striking area
is the fleshy part of the outside edge of
the hand. Avoid hitting with the wrist-
bone or the little finger bone when you
use the slash/block.

11

The slash is delivered with a cutting, whipping action. It can
be used in almost any direction--outward, upward, or down-
ward--and it can be delivered back-handed, cross-body and
double-handed. It can be aimed at high, low, or midrange
target areas.

This open-hand blow is utilized in many of the martial arts
and is known by dozens of names, including karate chop,
judo chop, jujitsu chop, knife-blade, sword-hand and the
Japanese word for it, *shuto*.

12   13

HAMMER BLOW

12, 13. As suggested by its name, the hammer blow is delivered with a pounding action. The striking point is the bottom of the closed fist.

The photos show a hammer blow delivered straight out. A downward hammer blow could also be delivered from the position shown in photo 12.

To deliver a side hammer blow, you would draw your fist cross-body and then hit back-handed.

BACK-KNUCKLE BLOW

This blow is delivered with the back of the two large knuckles. It is executed with a whipping action.

14. Bring your hand in close to your body and . . .

15. . . . deliver and up and outward back-knuckle blow as you draw your other hand back sharply.

ELBOW BLOW

16. The elbow blow is delivered by raising and bending the arm and hitting around and forward with the point of the elbow. Step as you hit and allow your upper body to follow the movement of your arm. The elbow blow is delivered with a smashing action.

14 15

16 17

STAB

17. The stabbing blow is delivered with the finger tips. Your thumb is held against the side of your hand. Unlike the hand position for the slash, the stabbing hand is held rigid. The blow is executed with a thrusting action.

18   19

SIDE STAMP & FORWARD STAMP

The stamps are power kicks performed with a smashing action.

18. To practice the side stamp, turn your weight-bearing foot outward at a 45-degree angle as you raise your kicking foot and . . .

19. . . . stamp to the side. Your foot is positioned parallel to the floor. The sole of your foot should be flat and it is aimed directly at the target.

20. To practice the forward stamp, raise your kicking foot and . . .

21. . . . stamp directly forward with the sole of your foot with your toes pointed upward.

SNAP KICK

The action of the snap kick is sharp and slashing.

22. Turn your weight-bearing foot at an angle as you raise your kicking foot with your sole turned inward and . . .

23. . . . snap your leg outward, kicking with the edge of your foot.

ROUNDHOUSE KICK

This kick is also called a circle kick or a hooking kick.

24, 25. As you turn your weight-bearing foot at an angle, draw your kicking leg up and back, positioning your foot horizontal to the floor, and deliver a high roundhouse, striking with the ball of the foot.

20

21

22

23

24

25

26

SLASH/BLOCK

26. The slashing block is executed with your open hand in the slash blow position. The striking area is anywhere along the arm and hand from the middle of the forearm to the outside edge of the hand. Do not hit with the wrist bone or the little finger bone.

The slashing block can be high or low, palm up or palm down, delivered outward or cross-body.

FOREARM BLOCKS

27. The forearm blocks will be described from a starting position as shown in this photo, with the blocking arm in a low guard.

28. From the low fist guard, draw your fist cross-body and block upward with your forearm parallel to the floor.

29. From the low fist guard, raise and bend your arm and block cross-body with the middle of your forearm.

30. From the guard position, raise and bend your arm and block outward with the middle of your forearm.

EXTENDED-ARM BLOCKS

31. From the low guard, hit cross-body with your fully extended arm, blocking with your forearm.

32. From the guard position, hit outward with your fully extended arm, blocking with your forearm.

27

28

29

30

31

32

33

TRAINING KATAS

To introduce the basic concept of combining various blows with foot and body movement, I have prepared two easy routines to help you learn and practice kata movements.

These can be done in solo practice, with a partner moving in unison, or they can be integrated into group practice sessions.

KATA "A"

33. Facing east, stand in a relaxed position with your body erect, but not tense. Your hands are loosely fisted at your thighs.

34. Without moving your right foot, step to the north with your left foot as you draw your right fist to your side, palm up, and block down with your left arm.

35. As you draw your left fist to your side, palm up, punch out with your right fist as you step forward with your right foot.

36. As you pivot on your left foot, step around clockwise with your right foot to face south and block down with your right arm.

34

35

36

37

38

39

37. Take a step forward with your left foot as you draw your right fist to your side and punch with your left fist.

38. Step counterclockwise with your left foot to face east and block down with your left arm.

39. Step forward with your right foot and execute a rising block with your right arm.

40. Step forward with your left foot and execute a rising block with your left arm.

41. Step forward with your right foot and execute a rising block with your right arm.

42. Pivot on your right foot and step around clockwise with your left foot to face south. Block down with your left arm as you draw your right fist to your side, palm up.

40   41

42

43

43. With your left foot in place, step to the west with your right foot and block down with your right arm as you draw your left fist to your side, palm up.

44

45

44. Take a step forward with your left foot as you block down with your left arm and draw your right fist to your side.

45. Take a step forward with your right foot as you block down with your right arm and draw your left fist to your side.

46. Pivot on your right foot and step around clockwise with your left foot to face north with your left foot advanced and execute a high forward slash with your left hand as you draw your right fist to your side.

47. With your left foot in place, step toward the northeast with your right foot as you deliver a high downward slash with your right hand and draw your left fist to your side.

48. Pivot on your left foot and step clockwise with your right foot to face south and deliver another high slash with your right hand.

46

47

48

49

50

49. With your right foot in place, step to the southeast with your left foot and slash with your left hand as you draw your right fist to your side.

50. Step back with your left foot to face east as you draw your left fist to your side.

†Resume the starting position as in photo 33.

This is the end of training kata A.

51

52

53

54

KATA "B"

51. From a relaxed standing position, step to the side with your right foot and assume a horse stance with your fists at your sides, palms up.

52. As you step forward with your right foot, deliver a rising block with your right arm.

53. As you step forward with your left foot, punch out with your left fist.

54. Without foot movement, draw your left fist to your side, punch with your right fist, and without hesitation ...

55

56

57

55. . . . execute a high kick with your right foot.

56. Recover with your right foot advanced and bring your right hand cross-body into a high slashing guard.

†Close your right hand, and then . . .

57. . . . execute a low outward block with your right arm.

58   59

60   61

58. Step forward with your left foot and draw your right fist to your side, palm up, and bring your left hand into a high slashing guard position.

59. Step forward with your right foot and execute a low, cross-body block with your right arm, as you draw your left fist to your side.

60. Assume a high slashing guard with your right hand as you open your left hand.

61. Take a step back with your right foot and assume a horse stance with your fists at your sides.

This is the end of training kata B.

62   63   64

PURPLE BELT—FIRST KATA

62. Assume a position of repose, facing east. Stand erect, but relaxed. Your lightly fisted hands are at your thighs. Your head is slightly lowered. This position is held for about five seconds.

63. Bow to the teacher (*sensei*).

64. Assume a position of attention. You stand straight and poised for movement. Your expression is alert and serious.

65. Pivot on the balls of your feet, turning counterclockwise to face north as you draw your right fist to your side, palm up, and block outward with your left forearm.

66. Stamp straight out to the north with your right foot as you punch with your right fist and draw your left fist to your side.

67. Swing your right leg around and pivot on your left foot to recover facing east in a horse stance with your fists at your sides.

68. Keeping your left foot in place, pivot on your right foot to face south and deliver an outward block with your right arm.

65

66

67

68

69   70   71

69. Deliver a stamping kick to the south with your left foot as you punch with your left fist and draw your right fist to your side.

70. Swing your left foot around and pivot on your right foot to recover into a horse stance facing east, with your fists at your sides.

71. Step forward with your right foot as you block upward with your right forearm.

72. Step forward with your left foot as you block upward with your left forearm.

73. Step forward with your right foot as you block upward with your right forearm.

74. Pivot on the balls of both feet to face north. Block downward with your left arm as you draw your right fist to your side.

72   73   74

75   76   77

75. Take a step to the north with your right foot as you punch high with your right fist and draw your left fist to your side.

76. Step with your left foot and pivot clockwise on your right foot, turning to face south as you prepare to . . .

77. . . . block downward with your left arm and draw your right fist to your side.

78   79   80

78. Step to the south with your right foot as you punch high with your right fist and draw your left fist to your side.

79. Step clockwise with your right foot and pivot on your left foot, turning to face west. As you block down with your right arm, draw your left fist to your side.

80. Take a step to the west with your left foot as you block down with your left arm and draw your right fist to your side.

81. Take a step to the west with your right foot as you block down with your right arm and draw your left fist to your side.

82. Preparing to make a three-quarter turn (to face north), pivot counterclockwise on your right foot and step around with your left foot . . .

83. . . . to complete the turn facing north with your left foot forward. You are in a slashing guard position and your right fist is at your side.

81 82 83

84 85 86

84. Take a step to the northeast with your right foot as you slash downward with your right hand and draw your left fist to your side.

85. Pivot on your left foot and step clockwise with your right foot . . .

86. . . . to face south in a slashing guard position with your left fist drawn to your side.

87

88

89

90

87. Take a step to the southeast with your left foot as you slash with your left hand and draw your right fist to your side.

88. Step back with your left foot to assume a horse stance facing east. Your fists are at your sides.

89. Return to the position of attention.

90. Bow.

†Return to the position of repose, as in photo 62.

This is the end of the purple belt first kata.

91   N   92

N   93   E   94

PURPLE BELT—SECOND KATA

†Start from the position of repose. Bow.

91. Assume the position of attention.

92. Pivot to face north as you block outward with your left forearm and draw your right fist to your side.

93. As you punch out with your right fist and draw your left fist to your side, execute a stamping kick with your right foot.

94. Swing your kicking leg around and pivot on your left foot to recover in a horse stance facing east and draw both fists to your sides.

S/E   95   96   97

98   99

95. Without foot movement, deliver a high punch to the southeast with your right fist as you block upward with your left forearm.

96. Step forward with your left foot and assume a high slashing guard position, placing your left hand palm down under your right elbow.

97. Step forward with your right foot as you assume a high slashing guard position with your right hand placed palm down under your left elbow.

98. Step forward with your left foot as you punch straight out with your left fist and draw your right fist to your side.

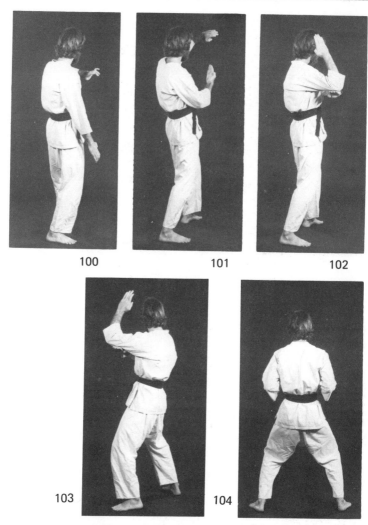

100

101

102

103

104

99. Step forward with your right foot and slash outward with your right hand as you place your left hand at your right elbow.

100. Pivot counterclockwise to face west and . . .

101. . . . slash upward with your left hand as you stab upward with your right hand, palm toward you.

102. Assume a high slashing guard, placing your left hand palm down under your right elbow.

103. Step forward with your right foot and assume a high slashing guard with your right hand under your left elbow.

104. Step forward with your left foot and assume a horse stance with your fists at your sides.

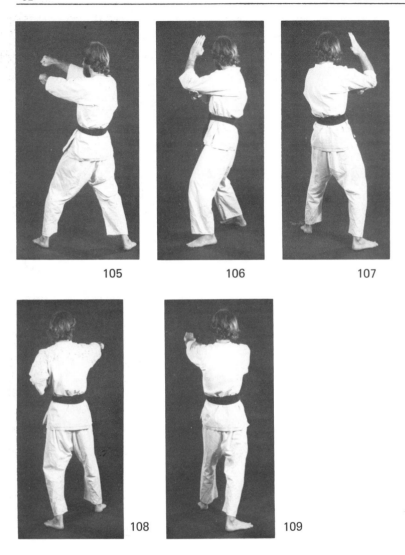

105. Without foot movement, block upward with your right forearm as you punch with your left fist.

106. Step back with your left foot and assume a high slashing guard, placing your right hand under your left elbow.

107. Step back with your right foot and assume a high slashing guard with your left hand under your right elbow.

108. Step forward with your right foot as you punch with your right fist and draw your left fist to your side.

109. Step forward with your left foot and slash outward with your left hand and place your right hand at your left elbow.

110 111 112

113 114

110,111. Pivot clockwise to face east and slash/block upward with your right hand as you stab up with your left hand.

112. Without foot movement, assume a high slashing guard, your left hand raised and your right hand under your left elbow.

113. Step forward with your left foot and assume a high slashing guard with your left hand under your right elbow.

114. Step forward with your right foot into a horse stance and draw your fists to your sides. † Assume the position of attention. Bow. Assume the position of repose. *This ends the second kata.*

115   116

PURPLE BELT—THIRD KATA

†Facing east, start from the position of repose. Bow. Assume the position of attention.

115. Step to the north with your left foot as you block outward with your left forearm and draw your right fist to your side.

116. Deliver a stamp kick to the north with your right foot as you punch with your right fist and draw your left fist to your side. Without putting your right foot on the floor, swing your right leg clockwise as you pivot on your left foot to . . .

117. . . . recover facing east in a horse stance and draw your right fist to your side.

118. Step back with your left foot as you block outward with your right forearm.

119. Step back with your right foot as you block downward with your left arm and draw your right fist to your side.

117 118 119

120 121 122

120. Step back with your left foot as you deliver a high back-knuckle blow with your right fist and draw your left fist to your side.

121. Pivot on your right foot and step clockwise with your left foot to face south. Assume a horse stance and execute a high crossed-arm block with your hands fisted.

122. Draw your fists to your sides.

123   124   125

123. Pivot on your left foot and step counterclockwise with your right foot to face north. Assume a horse stance and execute a crossed-arm high block with your hands fisted.

124. Draw your fists to your sides.

125. Pivot on your right foot to face east and draw your hands to your left side, fist-over-fist.

126. Step to the east with your left foot as you punch straight out with your left fist.

127. Step to the northeast with your right foot as you deliver a high elbow blow with your right arm and slap your right forearm with your left hand.

128. Pivot on both feet, turning counterclockwise to face west with your left foot advanced. Block upward with your left forearm as you draw your right fist to your side.

129. Block downward with your right arm as you draw your left fist to your side.

130. Deliver a back-knuckle blow with your right fist.

131. Pivot on your right foot and step around clockwise with your left foot to face east in a horse stance. Block upward with your arms crossed.

126 127 128

129 130 131

†Assume the position of attention. Bow. Assume the position of repose.

This is the end of the purple belt third kata.

132

133

134

135

PURPLE BELT—FOURTH KATA

†Start from a position of repose, facing east. Bow and then assume the position of attention.

132. Step to the north with your left foot and block outward with your left arm as you draw your right fist to your side.

133. Stamp kick with your right foot as you punch with your right fist and draw your left fist to your side. Without putting your foot on the floor, swing your right leg clockwise as you pivot on your left foot to . . .

134. . . . recover facing east in a horse stance as you draw your right fist to your side.

135. Punch down with both fists, bending your knees sharply.

136   137   138

139   140

136. Return to the horse stance with your arms crossed at your chest.

137. Deliver upward blocks with both arms.

†Draw your arms back to the crossed position at your chest.

138. Step forward with your right foot as you block upward with your right forearm and draw your left fist to your side.

139, 140. Take a step, crossing your right foot over your left foot as you start to shift hand position and then step to the west with your left foot. You are looking to the east with your hands at your left side, fist-over-fist.

141   142

141. Stamp kick to the northeast with your left foot as you deliver a downward hammer blow with your left fist and draw your right fist to your side.

142. Recover facing east with your left foot advanced. Punch down with your right fist as you draw your left fist to your side.

143. Step forward with your right foot as you deliver an elbow blow with your left arm and draw your right fist to your side.

144. Step forward with your left foot as you stab straight forward with your right hand and draw your left fist to your side.

145. Deliver an elbow blow with your left arm as you take a short step forward with your left foot and slap your left forearm with your right hand.

146. Step forward with your right foot and punch straight out with your right fist as you draw your left fist to your side.

147. Step back and out with your right foot to assume a horse stance with your fists at your side.

143   144   145

146   147

†Assume the position of attention. Bow. Assume the position of repose.

This is the end of the purple belt fourth kata.

148

149

150

151

PURPLE BELT—FIFTH KATA

†Assume the position of repose facing east. Bow. Assume the
position of attention.

148. Step to the north with your left foot and block outward
with your left forearm as you draw your right fist to your side.

149. Kick to the north with your right foot as you punch with
your right fist and draw your left fist to your side. Without
putting your foot on the floor, swing your right foot around
clockwise and pivot on your left foot to . . .

152   153

154   155

150. . . . recover facing east in a horse stance with your fists at your sides.

151. Punch down with both fists as you bend your knees sharply.

152. Rise and cross your arms at your chest.

153. Block upward with both arms.

†Cross your arms at your chest.

154. Punch to the south with your right fist and place your left hand palm down under your right upper arm.

155. Draw your right hand toward you and . . .

156   157

158   159   160

156. . . . deliver a back-knuckle blow with your right fist as you draw your left hand to your side, palm up.

157. Block downward with your left arm as you draw your right fist to your side.

158. Deliver a stamp kick to the northeast with your right foot as you punch with your fist and draw your left fist to your side.

159. Recover facing northeast with your right foot advanced and deliver an elbow blow with your left arm and draw your right fist to your side.

160. Block forward with your left forearm, as you draw your left hand to your side.

161 162 163

164 165

161. Pivot on both feet, turning counterclockwise to face west and bring your hands to your right side, fist-over-fist.

162, 163. Step to the west with your right foot, then take a step to the west with your left foot and pivot on both feet to face northeast with your hands at your left side, fist-over-fist.

164. Step to the north with your left foot and punch with your left fist as you draw your right fist to your side.

165. Step to the north with your right foot and deliver an elbow blow with your left arm and slap your left forearm with your right hand.

166   167   168

166. Step back with your right foot and place your left foot at your right knee as you block down with your left arm and draw your right fist to your side.

167. Place your left foot on the floor and block upward to the north with your left arm.

168, 169. Punch down with your right fist and quickly bring it back to your side.

170. Pivot on your right foot and step around clockwise with your left foot to face south with your left foot advanced, bearing weight on your right foot. Block up with your left arm as you draw your right open hand to your side.

171. Step clockwise with your left foot. Your body faces west. Look to the north and stab to the north with your right hand as you draw your left open hand to your side.

172. Step to the north with your right foot and deliver an elbow blow with your right arm as you slap your right forearm with your left hand.

169   170

171   172

†Step back counterclockwise with your right foot and face east. Assume the position of attention. Bow. Assume the position of repose.

This is the end of the purple belt kata series.

PRACTICING A WAZA

The first waza, which follows, is shown as it is performed
for demonstration, when both partners have learned their
separate movements and have worked out the timing so
that the routine is coordinated and lively.

In the purple belt wazas, there is a very brief hesitation
between each of the moves. In the brown belt waza series,
there is no hesitation; the routine movements are snappy,
continuous and brisk.

Both partners should learn both roles in all the wazas, that
of the "attacker" and that of the "defender."

Many of the movements in the wazas are simultaneous--
even when both partners are doing different movements,
they are doing them at the same time. To achieve smooth
simultaneous actions, partners must cooperate fully. As
you proceed to learn the various parts of the waza and practice them for technique and timing, you will work out the
subtle signs and movements that become your cues for
moving.

The most commonly used cue is a light tapping with both
hands at both thighs. The "defender" (shown at the left
side of the photos in all the waza series) gives the signal to
start.

PARTNERS

To develop skill in sparring and contest, it is useful to work
with a variety of different partners. To develop skill in
the performance of the wazas, it is best to work consistently
with a single partner

The objective of waza training is to achieve symmetry. One
of the partners should not look better than the other. If
one has problems with any of the movements, the other
partner should act as a helper and coach until the difficulty
is overcome.

NO CONTACT

There is no reason why people practicing wazas should risk injury since the best performance of the routines does not depend on near-contact blows, but on technical skill.

Except in the blocking and parrying moves, there is no contact. None of the hand or foot blows should come close to the body target. Unlike tournament karate, in which the controlled blow must come within a certain distance of the opponent in order to gain a point, the simulated blows in the waza series should leave enough distance so that the positions of both partners can be seen and judged for stance, balance, gesture and expressiveness.

In beginning practice, aim your hand and foot blows well out of contact range so that you do not make accidental contact. As you develop skill and control you should be able to aim your blows to within a few inches of the body target without making contact.

As an extra precaution, to avoid accidental contact at such vulnerable body areas as the eyes or the throat, do not aim your simulated hand and foot blows to them. Instead, aim at the forehead (rather than at the eyes) and at the chest (rather than at the throat). By taking these safety precautions, home study can be fun, exciting, and safe!

Although the waza is a mock assault/defense and counter, formalized and carefully arranged, there is *no* competition between the partners preparing for waza demonstration. To perform a waza with all the technique and dramatic gestures that mark a waza seen at its best, the partners have to cooperate totally and work hard in harmony.

With practice, you and your partner should be able to demonstrate the wazas with strong, appropriate gestures, simulating fast, technically perfect hit/block/counter actions, perfectly coordinated.

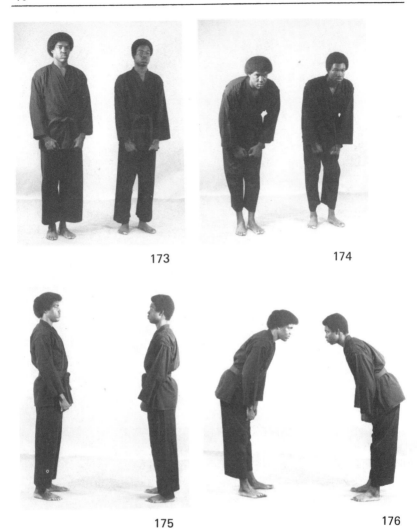

173

174

175

176

PURPLE BELT—FIRST WAZA

173. Partners walk to the starting area together, taking steps in unison, and assume the position of attention, facing the teacher (*sensei*).

174. They bow to the teacher in unison.

175. They face each other and each takes a step back in unison.

176. They bow to each other in unison, maintaining eye contact.

177. They assume the position of attention in unison.

177   178

179   180

178. As the left man sidesteps with his left foot and assumes
a horse stance, he fists his right hand and clasps it with his
left hand. Simultaneously the right man steps back with his
right foot and assumes a low guard position, leading with his
left fist. His fisted right hand is held at his side.

179. As the right man punches straight out with his right fist
and steps forward with his right foot, the left man steps back
clockwise with his right foot to assume a modified horse
stance and brings both fists to his side.

The right man maintains his position for the next three moves.

180. The left man steps in with his right foot and executes
a low right fist blow, followed by a . . .

181. . . . high right elbow blow as he slaps his right forearm with his left palm. Then he . . .

182. . . . steps back with his right foot and assumes a low guard, leading with his left fist.

183. As the left man steps forward with his right foot and assumes a horse stance, his hands held palm-over-fist, the right man steps back with his right foot and assumes a low guard, leading with his left fist.

184. In unison, they return to the position of attention.

This is the halfway point in the waza. The routine continues with a repetition of the foregoing moves, reversing right and left sides. To help you follow the instruction "reverse right and left sides," the following paragraphs will refer to the photos of the moves they are reversing.

†The left man sidesteps with his right foot and assumes a horse stance as he clasps his left fist with his right hand. The right man takes a step back with his left foot and assumes a low guard position, leading with his right fist. His right fist is at his side. (This is a reversal of photo 178.)

†As the right man punches straight out with his left fist and steps forward with his left foot, the left man steps back counterclockwise with his left foot into a modified horse stance and brings both fists to his sides, palm up. (This is a reversal of photo 179.)

The right man maintains his position for the next three moves.

†As the left man steps in with his left foot, he executes a low left fist blow (a reversal of photo 180) . . .

†. . . followed by a high left elbow blow, slapping his left forearm with his right palm. (A reversal of photo 181.)

†As the left man steps back with his left foot, he assumes a low guard, leading with his right fist. (A reversal of photo 182.)

†As the left man steps forward with his left foot and assumes a horse stance with his hands palm-over-fist, the right man steps back with his left foot and assumes a low guard, leading with his right fist. (A reversal of photo 183.)

†They return to the position of attention, as in photo 184

This is the end of the purple belt first waza.

181

182

183

184

185

186

PURPLE BELT—SECOND WAZA

†From the position of attention . . .

185. . . . as he sidesteps with his left foot, the left man assumes a horse stance with his hands in the palm-over-fist position. Simultaneously, the right man steps back with his right foot and assumes a low guard, leading with his left fist, with his right fist at his side.

186. The right man steps forward with his right foot and punches high with his right fist as he draws his left fist to his side. He maintains this position for the next two moves.

The left man parries the punch with his left hand, and steps clockwise with his right foot, drawing his right fist to his side.

187. The left man steps in with his right foot as he executes a high punch with his right fist and draws his left fist to his side, and then . . .

188. . . . steps back with his right foot and assumes a low guard leading with his left fist and draws his right fist to his side.

189. As the right man steps back with his right foot into a guard position leading with his left fist and his right fist at his side, the left man, without foot movement, assumes a guard position with his right fist overhead and his left fist low.

†The left man steps forward with his right foot, assumes a horse stance and brings his hands palm-over-fist, as in photo 185.

187

188

189

†Both return to the position of attention.

†This is the halfway point in the second waza. The routine continues as the moves are repeated, reversing right and left sides. Refer to photos 185 through 189.

†The left man returns to his position as in photo 185.

†Both return to the position of attention.

This is the end of the purple belt second waza.

PURPLE BELT—THIRD WAZA

†From the position of
attention . . .

190. . . . the right man steps
back with his right foot and
assumes a low guard, leading with his left fist, his
fisted right hand at his side.
Simultaneously, the left man
sidesteps with his left foot,
assuming a horse stance.
His hands are palm-over-
fist.

190

191

192

191. The right man steps forward with his right foot and
punches high with his right fist. He maintains this position
for the next two moves.

†As the right man punches, the left man takes a step with his
left foot and executes a slash/parry with his left hand as he
draws his right fist to his side.

192. The left man steps in with his right foot and executes
a high, back-handed slash as though to strike into the side of
the neck as he draws his left fist to his side, and then . . .

193

194

193. ... without foot movement, he executes a high palm-up slash, as though to strike into the side of the neck.

194. As the right man steps back with his right foot into a guard position leading with his left fist as he draws his right fist to his side, the left man steps back with his right foot, assuming a slashing guard with his right hand overhead.

†The right man maintains his position. The left man steps back with his left foot and takes a horse stance with his hands palm-over-fist.

†They return to the position of attention.

†They repeat the routine, reversing right and left sides.

†They return to the position of attention in unison.

This is the end of the purple belt third waza.

195

PURPLE BELT—FOURTH WAZA

†From the position of attention, the right man steps back with his right foot and assumes a low guard, leading with his left fist and with his right fist at his side. The right man assumes a horse stance with his hands palm-over-fist.

195. The right man punches straight out with his right fist as he steps forward with his right foot and draws his left fist to his side. As the right man punches, the left man steps back clockwise with his right foot as he draws both fists to his sides and then . . .

196. . . . steps forward with his right foot as he executes a heel-of-palm blow with his right hand and draws his left fist to his side. (The heel-of-palm blow is delivered with the fingers curled back as shown in the photo.) Then . . .

197. . . . without foot movement he executes a midsection punch with his right fist, and . . .

198. . . . as he steps back with his right foot, assuming a high/low guard position with his right hand in a heel-of-palm blow position overhead and his left fist low, the right man steps back with his right foot and assumes a guard position leading with his left fist and with his right fist at his side.

†The left man steps forward with his right foot and assumes a horse stance.

†In unison, both men return to the position of attention.

†They repeat the routine, reversing right and left sides.

†They return to the position of attention in unison.

This is the end of the purple belt fourth waza.

196

197

198

199

PURPLE BELT—FIFTH WAZA

†From the position of attention, the left man assumes the horse stance as the right man assumes the low guard leading with his left fist.

199. As the right man steps forward with his right foot, punches with his right fist, and draws his left fist to his side, the left man sidesteps and executes a block with his left forearm, then . . .

200. . . . steps forward with his right foot as he executes a high hammer blow with his right fist, and . . .

201. . . . without foot movement, executes a midsection punch with his right fist.

202. As the right man assumes the guard position leading with his left fist, the left man steps back into a guard position with his right fist high and his left fist low.

†They return to the position of attention.

†They repeat the routine, reversing right and left sides.

†They return to the position of attention.

This is the end of the purple belt fifth waza.

200

201

202

203   204

PURPLE BELT—SIXTH WAZA

†From the position of attention, the right man assumes a guard position, leading with his left fist as the left man assumes a horse stance.

203. The right man steps and punches as the left man sidesteps and cross-blocks with his left forearm and he draws his right fist to his side, then . . .

204. . . . steps forward with his right foot as he executes a "Y" hand blow (the striking point is at the base of the thumb and index fingers) and . . .

205. . . . without foot movement, executes a midsection punch with his right hand.

206. As the right man returns to his guard position, the left man steps back with his right foot into a guard, with his right hand high in the "Y" blow gesture and his left fist low.

†The left man assumes a horse stance.

†In unison, they return to the position of attention.

†They repeat the routine, reversing right and left sides.

†In unison they return to the position of attention.

207. They bow to each other.

208. They bow to the teacher (*sensei*) in unison.

†In unison they return to the position of attention.

This is the end of the purple belt waza series.

205

206

207

208

209

210

211

212

213

THIRD BROWN BELT—FIRST KATA

209. Start from the position of repose.

210. Bow.

211. Assume the position of attention.

212. Step to the north with your left foot as you raise your arms, in position to . . .

213. . . . block down with your left arm as you draw your right fist to your side.

214

215

216

217

218

214. Step forward with your right foot as you punch with your right fist and draw your left fist to your side.

215. Pivoting on both feet, turn clockwise 180 degrees to . . .

216. . . . face south with your right foot advanced. Block low with your right arm as you draw your left fist to your side.

217. Step forward with your left foot as you punch straight out with your left fist and draw your right fist to your side.

218. Take a step counterclockwise with your left foot to face east and block low with your left arm as you draw your right fist to your side.

219   220   221

219. Take a step forward with your right foot as you block up with your right forearm and draw your left fist to your side.

220. Step forward with your left foot as you block high with your left forearm and draw your right fist to your side.

221. Take a step forward with your right foot as you block high with your right forearm and draw your left fist to your side.

222. Pivot on both feet, turning counterclockwise to face west and continue turning, taking a step with your left foot to . . .

223. . . . face south as you block downward with your left arm and draw your right fist to your side.

224. Take a step with your right foot to face west and punch out with your right fist as you draw your left fist to your side.

225. Step forward with your left foot as you punch with your left fist and draw your right fist to your side.

226. Turning counterclockwise, make a three-quarter turn . . .

227. . . . to face north with your left foot advanced as you execute a high outward slash with your left hand and draw your open right hand to your side, palm up.

228. Take a step to the northeast with your right foot as you slash downward with your right hand and draw your left open hand to your side.

229. Pivot and step clockwise . . .

222

223

224

225

226

227

228

229

230

231

232   233   234

230. . . . to face south with your right foot advanced as you slash down with your right hand and draw your open left hand to your side.

231. Step to the southeast with your left foot as you slash with your left hand and draw your right hand to your side.

232. Step back with your left foot into a horse stance with your fists at your sides.

233. Bow

234. Return to the position of attention.

This is the end of the third brown belt first kata.

235

236

237

THIRD BROWN BELT—SECOND KATA

†Start from the position of repose, facing east. Bow. Assume the position of attention.

†Step to the side with your right foot and assume a horse stance with your fists at your sides.

235. Raise your right fist overhead, palm out as you look to the north and raise your left fist to shoulder height. *This is a slow movement.*

236. Deliver a fast uppercut blow with your right fist as you place your left fist at your right shoulder.

237. Deliver a side hammer blow with your left fist as you draw your right fist to your side.

238

239

240

241

238. Without foot movement, turn your upper body toward the south and raise your left fist overhead as you position your right fist at shoulder height. *This is a slow movement. All other movements in this kata are fast and vigorous.*

239. Deliver an uppercut with your left fist as you place your right fist at your left shoulder.

240. Deliver a side hammer blow with your right fist as you draw your left fist to your side.

241. Place the sole of your right foot at your left knee and draw your hands to your left side, fist-over-fist.

242

243

244

245

246

242. Deliver an edge-of-foot blow to the southwest as you execute a side hammer blow with your right fist.

243, 244. As you recover, step to the northeast with your left foot and slash with your left hand as you draw your right fist to your side.

245. Take a step to the southeast with your right foot as you slash with your right hand and draw your open left hand to your side.

246. Step to the northeast with your left foot as you slash with your left hand and draw your open right hand to your side, palm up.

247

248

249

250

251

247. Take a step to the east with your right foot as you stab
forward with your right hand and place your left hand, palm
down, under your right forearm.

248, 249. Pivot on your right foot and step clockwise with
your left foot to face south with your left foot advanced.
Slash with your left hand as you draw your open right hand to
your side.

250. Step to the southwest with your right foot as you slash
with your right hand and draw your left hand to your side.

251, 252. Pivot on your right foot and step around clockwise
with your left foot to face northwest. Slash with your left
hand as you draw your open right hand to your side.

252

253

254

255

256

253. Step to the north with your right foot as you slash with your right hand and draw your open left hand to your side.

254. Step to the west with your left foot as you swing your arms back and up.

255. Deliver a back-knuckle blow with your right fist as you draw your left fist to your side.

256. Deliver a stamping kick with your right foot.

257   258   259

257. As you recover with your right foot advanced, punch with your left fist as you draw your right fist to your side.

258. Swing your arms back and up.

259. Deliver a backhanded knuckle-blow with your left fist as you draw your right fist to your side.

260. Deliver a stamping kick with your left foot.

261. Recover facing southwest with your left foot advanced and punch with your right hand as you draw your left fist to your side.

262. Take a step to the southwest with your right foot as you block down with your right arm and draw your left fist to your side.

263. Pivot on your left foot and step around counterclockwise with your right foot to face north.

264. Step to the north with your left foot as you block upward with your left arm and draw your right fist to your side.

265. Pivot on both feet and turn your body clockwise to face south as you block down with your right arm and draw your left fist to your side.

260   261   262

263   264   265

266. Take a step to the southeast with your left foot as you block upward with your left arm and draw your right fist to your hip.

†Step back with your left foot to assume the horse stance with your fists at your sides. Assume the position of attention. Bow. Assume the position of repose.

This is the end of the third brown belt second kata.

266

267   268   269

THIRD BROWN BELT—THIRD KATA

†Assume the position of repose facing east. Bow. Assume the position of attention.

267. Take a step to the north with your left foot as you block outward with your left forearm and draw your right fist to your side.

268. Without arm movement, draw your right foot close to your left foot.

269. Snap your left fist down in a blocking action as you block up and outward with your right forearm.

270. Snap your right fist down in a blocking action as you block up and outward with your left forearm.

271. Pivot on your left foot and step around clockwise with your right foot to face south and block outward with your right arm as you draw your left fist to your side.

272. Without arm movement, draw your left foot close to your right foot.

273. Snap your right fist down in a blocking action as you block up and outward with your left forearm.

274. Snap your left fist down in a blocking action as you block up and outward with your right forearm.

275. Step to the east with your left foot and deliver a back-knuckle blow with your left fist as you draw your right fist to your side.

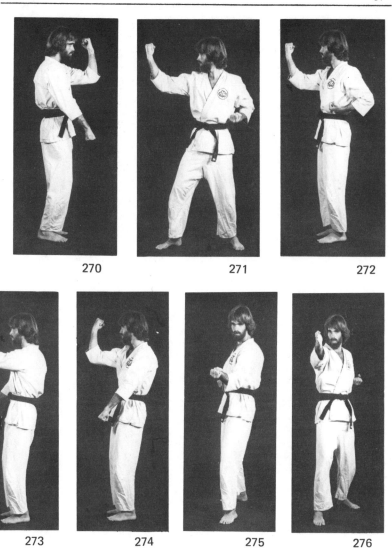

270   271   272

273   274   275   276

276. Step forward with your right foot as you stab straight out with your right hand and draw your left fist to your side.

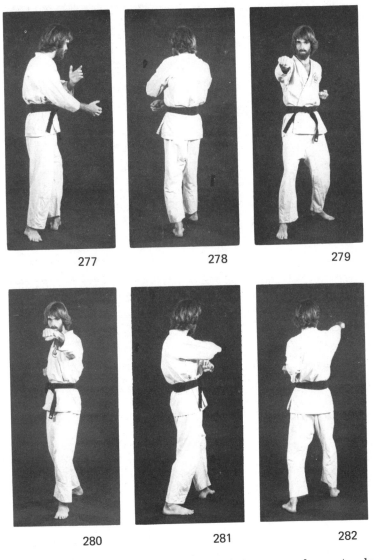

277   278   279

280   281   282

277-279. Pivot on your left foot and step around counterclockwise with your right foot to make a full turn and as you face
east, with your right foot advanced, punch with your right fist
and draw your left fist to your side. As you make the turn, open
your hands and make a circular movement, right hand over
left hand.

280. Step forward with your left foot as you punch with your
left fist and draw your right fist to your side.

281. Pivot on both feet, turning clockwise to face west as you
draw your fists in toward your chest, and then . . .

283

284

285

286

287

282. . . . take a step to the west with your right foot as you punch with your right fist and draw your left fist to your side.

283. Slide your left foot close to your right foot and place both fists at your sides, palms back.

284. Pivot on your left foot to face southwest and deliver a stamping kick with your right foot.

285, 286. Recover with your upper body facing southwest and your feet turned toward the south. Strike around counterclockwise with your right elbow.

287. Deliver a back-knuckle blow with your right fist.

288

289

290

291

288. Step around clockwise with your left foot to face west and place your fists at your sides, palms back.

289. Pivot on your right foot to face northwest and stamp-kick with your left foot.

290. As you recover, facing northwest, deliver an elbow blow with your left arm, followed by a . . .

291. . . . back-knuckle blow with your left fist.

292. Step around counterclockwise with your right foot to face west with your fists at your sides.

293. Step with your left foot and punch with your left fist.

292

293

294

295

296

294. Bring your right fist up to your left shoulder as you take a short step with your right foot and draw your left hand to your side.

295. Pivot on your right foot and step with your left foot, turning clockwise to face east.

296. Snap your right fist to your side as you bring your left fist to your right shoulder.

†Bring your left fist to your side as you assume a horse stance. Assume the position of attention. Bow. Assume the position of repose.

This is the end of the third brown belt third kata.

297   298   299

THIRD BROWN BELT — FOURTH KATA

†Start from the position of repose, facing east. Bow. Assume the position of attention. Take a horse stance with your fists at your sides.

297. Step to the north with your left foot as you assume a slashing guard with your right hand overhead and your left hand advanced.

298. Pivot on your right foot, turning to face south as you assume a high slashing guard with your left hand overhead and your right hand advanced.

299. Step to the northeast with your left foot and execute a low crossed-arm block with your hands fisted.

300. Take a step to the southeast with your right foot as you deliver an outward block with your right forearm and place your left fist at your right elbow.

301. Without moving your right foot, turn your body to the north, place your left foot at your right knee and draw your hands fist-over-fist to your right side.

300   301

302   303

302. As you deliver an edge-of-foot kick to the north, execute a back-knuckle blow with your left fist.

303. As you recover facing north with your left foot advanced, deliver an elbow blow with your right arm as you slap your right forearm with your left hand.

304

305

306   307   308

304. Pivot on your left foot, turning it to point east as you look toward the south; draw your right foot to your left knee and draw your hands fist-over-fist to your left side.

305. As you kick with an edge-of-foot blow to the south, deliver a back-knuckle blow with your right fist.

306. Recover with your feet pointed to the east; deliver an elbow blow to the south with your left arm as you slap your left forearm with your right hand.

307. Take a short step forward (to the east) with your right foot as you slash/block upward with your right hand and slash down with your left hand.

309

310

311

312

308. Stamp kick forward with your left foot as you draw your hands fist-over-fist to your right side.

309. Recover by placing your left foot down behind your right foot and deliver a back-knuckle blow with your right fist as you draw your left fist to your side.

310. Place the ball of your left foot lightly toward the northwest as you deliver a back-knuckle blow with your left fist and place your right fist at your left elbow.

311. Deliver a stamping kick to the northwest.

312. Recover with your left foot advanced and punch toward the northwest with your left fist as you draw your right fist to your side.

313. Without foot movement, punch to the northwest with your right fist as you draw your left fist to your side.

314. Pivot on your left foot and step counterclockwise on your right foot to face southwest with the ball of your right foot resting lightly on the floor and your weight on your left foot. Deliver a back-knuckle blow with your right fist as you place your left fist at your right elbow.

315. Deliver a stamping kick with your right foot.

316. Recover with your right foot advanced and punch to the southwest with your right fist as you draw your left fist to your side.

| 317 | 318 | 319 |

317. Without foot movement, punch with your left fist as you draw your right fist to your side.

318. Step to the southwest with your left foot as you deliver a back knuckle blow with your left fist and place your right fist at your left elbow.

319. Take a step to the northwest as you deliver a back-knuckle blow with your right fist and place your left fist under your right elbow.

320. Pivot on your left foot and step around counterclockwise with your right foot to face southeast with your right foot advanced and your arms raised, then . . .

320

321   322   323

321. . . . close your hands and pull down sharply as you hit up with your left knee.

322. Recover with your left foot advanced and slash toward the southeast with your left hand as you draw your open right hand to your side.

323. Pivot on your left foot and step around counterclockwise with your right foot to face northeast with your right foot advanced. Slash with your right hand as you draw your open left hand to your side.

†Step back with your right foot to face east in a horse stance. Your fists are at your sides. Assume the position of attention. Bow. Assume the position of attention.

This is the end of the third brown belt fourth kata.

324

325

THIRD BROWN BELT—FIFTH KATA

†Start from the position of repose, facing east. Bow. Assume the position of attention.

324. Step to the north with your left foot as you block outward with your left forearm and draw your right fist to your side.

325. Step forward with your right foot and punch with your right fist as you draw your left fist to your side.

326. Pivot on your left foot and step back clockwise with your right foot to face east and block outward with your right fist as you place your left fist at your right elbow.

327. Take a short step to the southeast and deliver a back-knuckle blow with your right fist as you draw your left fist to your side.

326

327

328   329   330

328. Without moving your right foot, pivot slightly on your left foot as you punch to the south with your left fist and draw your right fist to your side.

329. Face east and slide your left foot close to your right foot and extend your left forearm as you place your right fist at your left elbow.

330. Step forward with your right foot and block outward with your right arm as you place your left fist at your right elbow.

331. Step forward with your left foot and execute a downward crossed-arm block with your hands fisted.

332. Execute a high crossed-arm block with your hands open.

333. Draw your hands to your right side, fist-over-fist.

334. Draw your hands to your left side, fist-over-fist.

335. Punch forward with your left fist as you draw your right fist to your side.

336. Step forward with your right foot as you punch straight out with your right fist and draw your left fist to your side.

331   332   333

334   335   336

337   338   339

337. Pivot on your left foot and step to the south with your
right foot as you block low and outward with your right arm.

338. Pivot on both feet, turning counterclockwise to face
east with your left foot advanced and deliver a high slash to the
northeast with your left hand as you draw your right hand to
your side.

339. Deliver a high kick toward the northeast with your right
foot as you slap the foot with your left hand and shout *a ki ai.*

340. Recover with your right foot advanced, hit forward with
your right elbow and slap your forearm with your left hand.

341. Draw your left foot to your right foot, weight resting
lightly on the ball of your left foot and deliver a back-knuckle
blow with your right fist as you place your left fist at your
right elbow.

342. Pivot on your right foot and step with your left foot to
face west with your right fist in a high guard and your left fist
under your right elbow.

340   341   342

343   344   345

343-345. Making a counterclockwise 180-degree turn, first step around with your right foot as you pivot on your left foot; when your right foot is on the floor, pointed south, take a step with your left foot, crossing it behind your right foot; pivot your right foot to point southeast as you bend your crossed legs and block downward with crossed arms.

346   347

346. As you rise, pivot on your left foot and step toward the southwest with your right foot and deliver a back-knuckle blow with your right fist as you place your left fist at your right elbow.

347. Pivot on both feet to face southeast and stab down with your right hand palm up as you shift your weight forward and bend your knees and place your left hand palm up at your right shoulder.

348. As you rise from the bent-knee position and shift your weight back, block down with your left arm as you draw your right fist to your side.

349. Step forward with your right foot and stab down with your left hand palm up, knees bent, as you place your right hand at your left shoulder, palm up.

350. As you rise from the bent-knee position and shift your weight back, block down with your right fist and draw your left fist to your side.

348

349

350

351

351. Step back with your right foot into a horse stance with your fists at your sides.

†Assume the position of attention. Bow. Assume the position of repose.

This is the end of the third brown belt kata series.

352

THIRD BROWN BELT—FIRST WAZA

†In unison, the partners walk to the starting area and they assume the position of attention, facing the teacher. For the purpose of following the instruction in the text, they will be facing east. They bow to the teacher. They face each other and each takes a step back. They bow to each other, maintaining eye contact. They assume the position of attention,352.

353. The left man takes a step to the side with his left foot and assumes a horse stance with his fists at his thighs, as the right man steps back with his right foot into a guard position with his left fist low and his right fist at his side.

354. The right man steps forward with his right foot and punches low with his right fist as he draws his left fist back, palm up. As the right man punches, the left man steps forward with his left foot as he blocks outward with his left arm and draws his right fist to his side, and . . .

355. . . . without foot movement, he punches high with his right fist as he draws his left fist to his side.

356. As the left man returns to the horse stance with his fists at his thighs, the right man steps back with his right foot into the guard position with his left fist low.

†They return to the position of attention.

†They repeat the movements, reversing right and left sides.

†In unison, they return to the position of attention.

This is the end of the third brown belt first waza.

353

354

355

356

357

358

THIRD BROWN BELT—SECOND WAZA

†From the position of attention, the left man assumes a horse stance with his fisted hands at his thighs as the right man assumes the low guard with his left foot and left fist forward.

357. As the right man steps forward and punches high with his right fist, drawing his left fist back, the left man steps forward with his left foot and executes an outward forearm block as he draws his right fist to his side, and . . .

358. . . . without foot movement, he punches with his right fist as he draws his left fist to his side.

†They return to the position of attention.

†They repeat the movements, reversing right and left sides.

†They return to the position of attention.

This is the end of the third brown belt second waza.

359

360

THIRD BROWN BELT—THIRD WAZA

†From the position of attention, the left man assumes the horse stance as the right man assumes the low left guard.

359. As the right man steps forward with his right foot and punches high with his right fist, the left man steps in with his left foot, executes a high slashing block and draws his right fist to his side. Then . . .

360. . . . without foot movement, he stabs straight out with his right hand as he draws his left fist to his side.

†In unison, they return to the position of attention.

†They repeat the movements, reversing right and left sides.

†In unison, they return to the position of attention.

This is the end of the third brown belt third waza.

361

362

363

THIRD BROWN BELT—FOURTH WAZA

†From the position of attention, the left man assumes the horse stance as the right man assumes his low guard position.

361. As the right man steps forward with his right foot and punches high, the left man steps in with his left foot and executes a high slashing block with his left hand, and then . . .

362,363. . . . grips the sleeve of the punching arm and pulls the right man forward, executing a punch with his right fist.

†They return to the position of attention, then repeat the movements, reversing right and left sides.

†They return to the position of attention.

This is the end of the third brown belt fourth waza.

364

365

THIRD BROWN BELT—FIFTH WAZA

†From the position of attention, the left man assumes a horse stance as the right man assumes the low left guard.

364. As the right man steps and punches with his right fist, the left man steps in with his left foot and blocks upward with his left forearm and then . . .

365. . . . executes a straight out punch with his right fist.

†They return to the position of attention.

†They repeat the movement, reversing right and left sides.

†In unison, they return to the position of attention.

This is the end of the third brown belt fifth waza.

366   367

THIRD BROWN BELT—SIXTH WAZA

†From the position of attention, the right man steps into the low left guard as the left man assumes a horse stance.

366. As the right man steps and punches with his right fist, the left man sidesteps with his left foot and executes a cross-body block with his left forearm, and then . . .

367. . . . punches with his right fist as he draws his left fist to his side.

†In unison they return to the position of attention.

†They repeat the movements, reversing right and left sides.

368. In unison, they return to the position of attention.

†In unison, they bow to each other. They turn to face the teacher and bow. They return to the position of attention.

This is the end of the third brown belt waza series.

368

369

370

SECOND BROWN BELT—FIRST WAZA

†In unison, partners walk to the starting area and assume the position of attention, facing the teacher (east). They bow to the teacher. They face each other. Each takes a step back and . . .

369. . . . they bow to each other, then . . .

† . . . return to the position of attention.

370. In unison, both men assume a low left guard, leading with the left fist and foot and the right fist drawn back, palm up.

371   372

373

371. As the right man steps forward with his right foot,
punches with his right fist and draws his left fist back,
palm up, the left man blocks downward and outward with his
left arm as he takes a short step with his left foot and shifts
his weight forward. Without foot movement, the left man . . .

372. . . . punches straight out with his right fist as he draws
his left fist to his side.

373. Both men return to the low left guard position in
unison.

†They assume the position of attention.

†They repeat the waza, reversing right and left sides.

This is the end of the second brown belt first waza.

374

375

376

SECOND BROWN BELT—SECOND WAZA

†From the position of attention, both men assume a low left guard in unison.

374. The right man steps forward with his right foot as he punches with his right fist, as the left man takes a short step forward with his left foot, blocking cross-body with his left forearm, and without changing his foot position . . .

375. . . . punches with his right fist as he draws his left fist back, and then . . .

376. . . . shifts his weight forward as he executes a high blow with his left elbow.

†Both men return to the low left guard in unison. They return to the position of attention.

†They repeat the routine, reversing right and left sides.

This is the end of the second brown belt second waza.

377   378

SECOND BROWN BELT—THIRD WAZA

†From the position of attention, both men assume a low left guard, in unison.

377. As the right man steps and punches, the left man takes a short step in with his left foot and executes a high, outward slashing block and opens his right hand. Then he . . .

378. . . . shifts his weight forward as he executes a slashing blow, palm up, with his right hand, followed by a . . .

379. . . . palm-up slashing blow with his left hand as he draws his right open hand to his side.

379

†Both men assume a low left guard in unison. They return to the position of attention.

†They repeat the waza, reversing right and left sides.

This is the end of the second brown belt third waza.

380

381

382

SECOND BROWN BELT—FOURTH WAZA

†From the position of attention, both men assume a low left guard in unison.

380. As the right man punches with his right fist and steps with his right foot, the left man shifts his weight forward and executes a high outward block with his left forearm, then . . .

381. . . . kicks into the midsection with his right foot, then . . .

382. . . . punches with his right fist as he places his kicking foot onto the floor.

†They return to the low left guard position in unison. They return to the position of attention.

†They repeat the waza, reversing right and left sides.

This is the end of the second brown belt fourth waza

383

384

385

SECOND BROWN BELT—FIFTH WAZA

†From the position of attention, both men assume a low left guard in unison.

383. As the right man steps and punches, the . . .

384. . . . left man ducks down and starts to turn counter-clockwise and . . .

385. . . . executes a high, circle kick with his right foot. He rises to face his partner.

†Both men assume a low left guard position in unison. They return to the position of attention.

†They repeat the waza, reversing right and left sides.

This is the end of the second brown belt fifth waza.

386

387

SECOND BROWN BELT—SIXTH WAZA

386. From the position of attention, the left man steps back into a low left guard as the right man steps back with his right foot and draws both fists to his sides.

387. The right man punches forward with both fists.

388

389

388, 389. As the right man punches, the left man raises both
fists and executes a double downward and outward block,
and then . . .

390

391

390. . . . grips both sleeves just above the elbows, and . . .

391. . . . pulls his opponent partner toward him as he executes a knee kick.

†Both men return to the positions in photo 386. They return to the position of attention.

†They repeat the waza, reversing right and left sides.

This is the end of the second brown belt sixth waza.

392

393

394

SECOND BROWN BELT—SEVENTH WAZA

†From the position of attention, both men assume a low left guard in unison.

392. The right man steps and punches high with his right fist as the left man sidesteps and blocks with his left forearm, and then . . .

393. . . . punches into the midsection with his right hand as he draws his left fist back.

394. The right man blocks with his left arm as he draws his right fist back, and then . . .

395

396

397

395. . . . delivers a right punch, which is . . .

396. . . . blocked upward by the left man. As the block is executed, each draws the unengaged fist to his side.

397. The left man executes an upward punch.

†They return to the guard position in unison. They return to the position of attention.

†They repeat the waza, reversing right and left sides.

This is the end of the second brown belt seventh waza.

398

399

SECOND BROWN BELT—EIGHTH WAZA

†From the position of attention, both men assume a low left guard in unison.

398. As the right man steps and executes a back-knuckle blow, the left man blocks upward with his left forearm, then he . . .

399. . . . grips cloth at the upper sleeve, and pulls his opponent partner forward as he executes a straight out punch with his right fist.

†They return to the low left guard in unison. They return to the position of attention.

†They repeat the waza, reversing right and left sides.

This is the end of the second brown belt eighth waza.

400

401

402

SECOND BROWN BELT — NINTH WAZA

†From the position of attention, both men assume the low left fist guard in unison.

400. The right man steps and punches high with his right fist as the left man executes a high slashing block, and then . . .

401. . . . grips cloth high at the sleeve and . . .

402. . . . pulls his opponent partner forward as he delivers a straight out fist blow.

403

404

403. The right man blocks upward with his left forearm and begins a circle kick, which the . . .

404. . . . left man blocks with his right arm.

†They return to the guard position in unison. They return to the position of attention.

†They repeat the waza reversing right and left sides.

This is the end of the second brown belt ninth waza.

405

406

SECOND BROWN BELT—TENTH WAZA

†From the position of attention, both men assume a low left guard in unison.

405. As the right man steps and punches, the left man blocks the punch with his left palm then he . . .

406. . . . grips the wrist and . . .

407. . . . pulls his opponent partner forward as he delivers a circle kick with his right foot.

†They return to the guard position in unison. They return to the position of attention

†They repeat the waza reversing right and left sides.

This is the end of the second brown belt tenth waza.

407

408

409

SECOND BROWN BELT—ELEVENTH WAZA

†From the position of attention, both men assume a low left guard in unison.

408. The right man executes a circle kick with his right foot, which the left man blocks with his left arm. Then he . . .

409. . . . punches with his right fist.

410

411

412

410. The right man blocks upward with his left forearm, and . . .

411. . . . delivers a right punch straight out as he draws his left fist back.

412. The left man blocks the punch outward with his left arm.

†They return to the guard position and then to the position of attention.

†They repeat the waza reversing right and left sides.

This is the end of the second brown belt eleventh waza.

413

414

SECOND BROWN BELT—TWELFTH WAZA

†From the position of attention, both men assume a low left guard in unison.

413. The right man steps and punches as the left man sidesteps and blocks cross-body with his left forearm and then . . .

414. . . . starts a forward toe kick with his right foot as he brings his fists to his hips. The right man crosses his fists, in preparation to . . .

415

416

415. . . . cross-arm block the kick. Then he . . .

416. . . . counters with a circle kick with his right foot
as he draws his fists to his sides. The left man blocks the kick
with his left arm.

417

418

†Both men return to the low left guard in unison.

†They repeat the waza, reversing right and left sides.

417. In unison, they return to the low left guard.

†In unison, they bow to the teacher.

418. They face each other and bow. They assume the position of attention.

This is the end of the second brown belt waza series.

419   420   421

FIRST BROWN BELT KATA

There is only a single kata for the first brown belt, but it is
a long routine. Unlike most other katas, this one consists of
fast and slow movements. Ordinarily, katas are composed of
fast movements or slow movements only.

The fast actions are performed with snap, drive and gestures
of power. The slow movements are performed with exaggerated,
dramatic precision. They are graceful and elegant, but retain
a feeling of strength.

Up to the movement shown in photo 442, all the movements
are fast. After that, fast movements will be indicated by (f)
and slow movements by (s).

419. From the position of attention, bow.

†Return to the position of attention.

420. Assume a horse stance with your fists at your sides,
palms up.

421. Take a step forward with your right foot and punch with
your left fist.

422

423

424

425

426

422. Take a step forward with your left foot and punch out with your right fist as you draw your left fist to your side.

423. Step forward with your right foot as you block upward with your right forearm, drawing your left fist to your side.

424. As you step forward with your left foot, block up with your left forearm as you draw your right fist to your side.

425. Pivot counterclockwise on your left foot to . . .

426. . . . face west with your right foot advanced. Block down with your right arm as you draw your left fist to your side.

427   428

429   430

427. Swinging your right leg and pivoting on your left foot . . .

428. . . . make a complete 360-degree counterclockwise turn to face west with your right foot advanced and block down with your right arm as you draw your left fist to your side.

429. Pivot and step counterclockwise to face south, leading with your right foot. Slash forward with your left hand and draw your right open hand to your side.

430. Pivot on your right foot and step clockwise with your left foot to face north, leading with your left foot. Slash with your right hand and bring your open left hand to your side.

431   432   433

434   435

431. Step counterclockwise with your right foot to face west. Punch with your right hand as you draw your left fist to your side.

432. Deliver a stamping kick with your right foot.

433. As you place your right foot down, punch with your left hand and draw your right fist to your side.

434. Deliver a stamping kick with your left foot.

435. As you place your left foot down, punch with your right fist and draw your left fist to your side.

436

437

438

439

440

436. Pivot on the ball of your left foot and step around counterclockwise with your right foot to . . .

437. . . . face northeast. During the turn, your hands are held palm out and make a sweeping movement with the turn. Hesitate briefly.

438. As you draw your open left hand to your side, slash outward with your right hand.

439. Pivot on your right foot and step with your left foot to . . .

440. . . . face southeast, leading with your left foot and your open hands held palm out. Hesitate briefly.

441   442   443

444   445   446

441. As you slash forward with your left hand, draw your right open hand to your side.

442. *This is the first of the slow movements.* Pivot on your left foot and step around counterclockwise with your right foot to . . .

443. . . . face northeast. In slow motion, but with a feeling of strength and control, place your right foot on the floor as you extend your right fist and draw your left fist to your side.

444. Without moving the rest of your body, turn your head to look southeast and point your right foot to the southeast (s).

445. Pivot on your right foot and step clockwise with your left foot to . . .

446. . . . face southeast, leading with your left foot, your right hand extended in a slashing gesture and your open left hand drawn to your side (s). Hesitate.

447. Punch with your left hand as you draw your right fist to your side (s).

448. Without moving the rest of your body, look to the northeast and turn your left foot to the northeast (s).

447

448

449

449. Pivot on your left foot and step around counterclockwise with your right foot to face northeast with your left hand in a slashing gesture and your right open hand drawn to your side (s).

450. Without stepping, pivot on both feet turning counterclockwise to face west. Both hands are in a slashing gesture, your right hand is overhead (s).

450

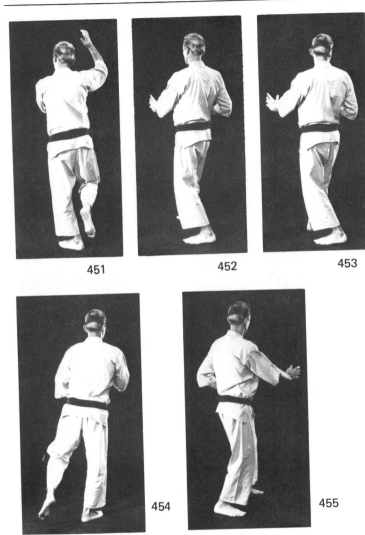

451

452

453

454

455

451. Step with your right foot (s) . . .

452. . . . to face southwest, leading with your right foot, your left hand in a slashing gesture and your open right hand drawn to your side (s).

453. Without body movement, turn your right foot and look toward the northwest (s).

454. Step clockwise with your left foot (s) . . .

455. . . . to face northwest with your left foot advanced, your right hand in a slashing gesture and your open left hand drawn to your side (s).

456 457

458 459 460

456. Pivot on your left foot and slowly swing your arms outward to your right side, as you begin to (s) . . .

457. . . . turn counterclockwise, stepping with your right foot (s) to . . .

458. . . . face southeast, leading with your right foot, your left hand in a slashing gesture and your right hand drawn to your side (s).

459. Turn your right foot toward the southwest and look to the southwest (s).

460. Pivot on your right foot and step around clockwise with your left foot (s) to . . .

461

462

463

464

465

466

461. . . . face southwest, leading with your left foot, your right hand forward in a slashing gesture and your left hand drawn to your side (s).

462. Turn your head to look east as you begin to (s) . . .

463. . . . pivot on your left foot and step around clockwise with your right foot . . . *(fast movements follow)*

464. . . . to face east, leading with your right foot. As you put your foot down, deliver a fast, vigorous back-knuckle blow with your right fist as you draw your left fist to your side.

465. Deliver a high stamp kick with your right foot (f).

467

468

469

470

466. Recover with your right foot advanced and block outward with both forearms (f).

467. As you step to the southeast with your right foot, punch to the southeast with your left fist and draw your right fist to your side (f).

468. Step forward with your left foot and punch to the southeast with your right fist (f).

469. Step forward with your right foot into a horse stance with your fists at your sides (f) . . .

470. . . . then pivot and step, turning counterclockwise 180 degrees to face west, leading with your right foot, and block down with your right arm (f).

471   472

473   474

471. Step with your left foot into a horse stance with your fists at your sides (f).

472. Step to the northwest with your right foot and block outward with your right forearm (f).

473. With your left foot in place, take another step with your right foot and punch with your left fist as you draw your right fist to your side (f).

474. Take a step to the southwest with your left foot and block outward with your left forearm as you draw your right fist to your side (f).

475 476

477 478

475. With your right foot in place, take another step with your left foot as you punch with your right fist and draw your left fist to your side (f).

476. Take a step with your right foot into a horse stance with your fists at your sides (f).

477. Pivot on your right foot and step around clockwise to face east, leading with your left foot and block down with your left arm (f).

478. Step forward with your right foot to assume a horse stance with both fists at your sides (f).

479   480

481   482   483

479. *Slow movements follow.* Stand erect as you extend your arms outward, palms down (s).

480. Draw your right foot back to your left foot, bearing weight on your left foot and cross your arms with your hands open (s).

481. Take a short step forward with your right foot and bring your right hand to a high slashing guard position (s).

482. Draw your left foot back, bearing weight on your right foot and cross your arms with your hands open (s).

484   485

486   487

483. Take a short step forward with your left foot and bring your left hand into a high slashing guard position and position your open right hand in front of your chest, palm up (s).

484, 485. Pivot counterclockwise on your left foot and slowly swing your right leg around . . .

486. . . . to make a 180-degree turn to face west, leading with your right foot and block downward with your right arm as you draw your left fist to your side (s).

487. Step with your left foot and assume a horse stance with your fists at your sides (s).

488   489   490

Fast and slow movements follow.

488. Step to the northwest with your right foot and slash with your right hand (f).

489. Pivot on your left foot and step with your right foot to face south. Assume a horse stance with your fists at your sides (s).

490. Step to the southwest with your right foot and slash with your right hand as you open your left hand (f).

491. Step to the southeast with your left foot and slash with your left hand as you draw your open right hand to your side (f).

492. Pivot on your left foot and step counterclockwise with your right foot to face north in a horse stance with your fists at your sides (s).

493. Step to the northwest with your left foot and slash with your left hand, opening your right hand (f).

494. Step to the northeast with your right foot and slash with your right hand as you draw your open left hand to your side (f).

491 492 493

494 495 496

495. With your left foot in place step with your right foot to face east and slash/block low with your right hand (f).

496. Step with your left foot and slash/block low with your left hand as you draw your open right hand to your side (f).

497

498

499

500

501

497. Step with your right foot into a horse stance with your fists at your sides (s).

Fast movements follow.

498. Pivot on your left foot and step clockwise with your right foot to face west and block outward with your right forearm (f).

499. Without foot movement, block downward with your right arm (f).

500. Take a step to the west with your left foot and block outward with your left forearm as you draw your right fist to your side (f).

502

503

504

505

501. Without foot movement, block downward with your left arm (f).

502. Deliver a leaping stamp kick with your right foot, and . . .

503. . . . recover with your right foot advanced. Deliver an elbow blow with your right arm as you slap your right forearm with your left hand (f).

504. Without stepping, pivot on both feet, turning counter-clockwise to face east, leading with your left foot and block upward with your left forearm as you draw your right fist to your side (f).

505. Without foot movement, block down with your left arm (f).

506

507

508

509

506. Pivoting on your left foot, using your right leg as a counterweight, turn counterclockwise (f) . . .

507. . . . making a full circle to face east and squat, leading with your left foot, slapping the floor with your right hand (f) and without hesitation . . .

508. . . . spring up and deliver a leaping stamp kick with your right foot (f).

509. Recover with your right foot forward and block upward with crossed arms (f).

510. Step counterclockwise with your right foot to face north, leading with your right foot and block up with your right forearm (f).

510

511

512

513

514

511. Without foot movement, punch with your left fist as you draw your right fist to your side (f).

512. Pivot on your left foot and step counterclockwise to face west, leading with your right foot and slash upward with your right hand as you draw your open left hand to your side (f).

513. Without foot movement, punch with your left fist as you draw your right hand to your side (f).

514. Pivot on your left foot and step with your right foot to face south and slash upward with your right hand as you draw your open left hand to your side (f).

515

516

517

518

515. Without foot movement, punch with your left fist as you draw your right fist to your side (f).

516. With your right foot in place, step with your left foot to face east and deliver a back-handed knuckle blow with your left fist (f).

517. Stamp kick with your right foot and punch with your right hand as you draw your left fist to your side (f).

†Assume a horse stance with your fists at your side (s).

†Slowly bow.

518. Slowly return to the position of attention.

This ends the first brown belt kata.

519

520

521

BLACK BELT—FIRST KATA

Black belt kata performance is expected to demonstrate a singularly high level of technical excellence. The black belt series of katas is performed in very slow motion. When the movements are slow, every nuance of technique is revealed. In slow motion, hand, foot and body position must be perfectly coordinated to maintain balance and control.

Each move is done with flowing, strong gestures. The movements are graceful, but they suggest disciplined power. The position of each hand and foot blow, parry and block, pivot and turn, must accurately represent the action even though it is done slowly.

Between each posture there is a slight hesitation.

†From the position of repose, facing east, bow, then assume the position of attention.

519. Step to the side with your right foot so that your feet are about shoulder-width apart. Bow your head and place your hands in front of you, palms down. This is the meditative stance.

520. Assume a horse stance with your fists at your sides.

521. Step forward with your right foot, perform a crossed-arm block overhead with your hands open. There will be no foot movement for the next ten moves.

522   523   524

522. Block outward with both forearms, your open hands held palms toward you.

523. As you draw your right open hand to your side, slash upward with your left hand.

524. Draw your left hand to your side. Make fists, palms up.

525. Parry cross-body with your left hand.

†Draw your fists to your sides, as in photo 524.

526. Slash forward with your left hand as you open your right hand.

†Draw your left hand to your side and fist both hands as in photo 524.

527. Assume a stylized blocking guard position with your right hand raised, palm up and your left hand lowered, palm down.

528. As you draw your open right hand to your side, block outward with your left forearm, your hand palm up.

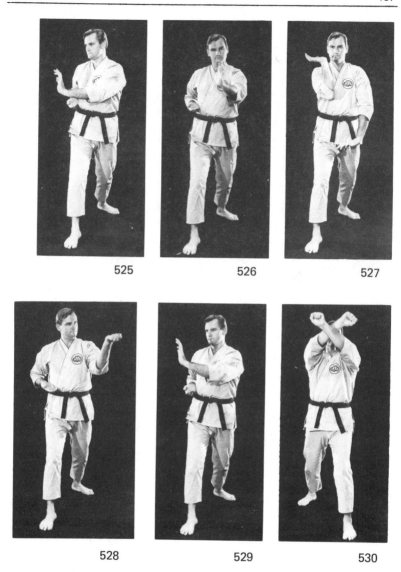

525

526

527

528

529

530

529. Parry cross-body with your left hand.

530. Step forward with your left foot and block upward with your arms crossed, your hands fisted.

531   532   533

534   535   536

531. As you draw your left open hand to your side, deliver a high outward block with your right forearm.

532. Deliver a low outward slashing-block with your right hand.

533. Step forward with your right foot as you block upward with open hands with your arms crossed.

534. Make a circular movement with your hands and extend your arms forward, palms up.

535. Draw your fists to your sides.

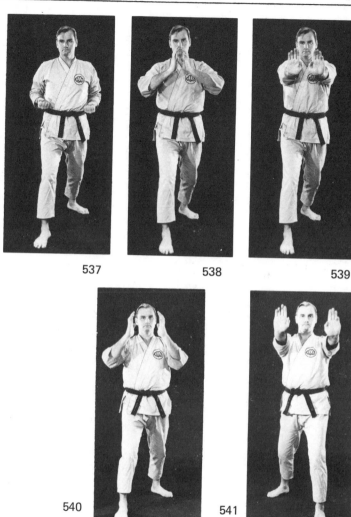

537 538 539

540 541

536, 537. *This is a fast movement, the only one in the black belt kata series, accompanied by a voiced ki-ai.* Bring your open hands together, palms up, and then quickly bring your fists to your sides.

538. Bring your open hands together, palms facing.

539. Extend your arms forward, palms out.

†Draw your fists to your sides, as in photo 537.

540. Raise your open hands, palms facing.

541. Step back with your right foot as you extend both arms, palms forward.

542

543

544

545

546

542. Bring your fists to your sides.

543. Raise your open hands, palms facing.

544. Step back with your left foot as you extend your arms, palms forward.

545. Assume the stylized guard position with your right hand raised, palm up, and your left hand low, palm down.

†Bring your fists to your sides as you step back with your right foot to assume a horse stance.

546. Assume the meditative stance.

This is the end of the black belt first kata.

BLACK BELT — SECOND KATA

All movements are in slow motion.

†Assume the position of repose, facing
east. Bow. Assume the position of
attention. Assume the position of meditation. Assume a horse stance with
your fists at your sides.

547. Step forward with your left foot
and raise your left fist to a guard
position and draw your right fist to your
side.

547

548   549   550

548. Block downward with your right arm as you draw your
left fist to your side.

†Draw your right fist to your side and raise your left fist in
the guard position as in photo 547.

549. Punch forward with your right fist as you draw your left
fist to your side.

†Draw your right fist to your side and assume the guard
position as in photo 547.

550. Block downward with your left arm.

        551   552   553

551. Block outward with your left forearm.

552. Step forward with your right foot and draw your left fist to your side as you raise your right fist in a guard position.

553. Block down and outward with your left arm as you draw your right fist to your side.

†Draw your left fist to your side as you raise your right fist in the guard position, as in photo 552.

554. Punch forward with your left fist as you draw your right fist to your side.

†Draw your left fist to your side and assume the guard position as in photo 552.

555. Block down and outward with your right arm.

556. Block up and outward with your right forearm.

557. Step forward with your left foot, draw your right open hand to your side, palm up, and raise your left hand in a slash/guard position.

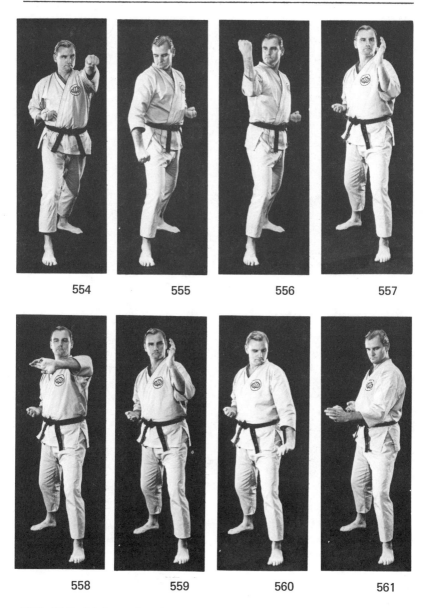

554 555 556 557

558 559 560 561

558, 559. Make a circular movement with your left hand, thumb down, palm out, continuing the circular movement to bring your left hand in a slash/guard position.

560. Slash/block down with your left hand.

561. Parry cross-body with your left had.

562   563   564

565   566   567

562. Raise your left hand into a slash/guard position.

563. As you draw your left open hand to your side, slash/block down and outward with your right hand.

564. Draw your right elbow back and then stab straight forward with your right hand.

565. Step forward with your right foot and bring your right hand into a slashing guard position.

566, 567. Make a circular movement with your right open hand, and bring it to the slashing guard position.

568

569

570

571

572

568. Slash/block down with your right hand.

569. Parry cross-body with your right hand.

†Bring your right hand to the slashing guard position, as in photo 567.

570. As you draw your right open hand to your side, palm up, slash/block down with your left hand.

571. Draw your left elbow back and then stab forward with your left hand.

572. As you draw your left open hand to your side, raise your right hand to a slash/guard position.

573   574   575   576

573. Place your left open hand palm down under your right wrist.

574. Stab forward with your right hand as you slide your left hand under your upper arm and take a step forward with your left foot.

575. Reverse your hand position and place your right hand palm down under your left wrist, then . . .

576. . . . step forward with your right foot as you stab forward with your left hand and slide your right hand back under your upper arm.

†Step back with your right foot and assume a horse stance with your fists at your sides. Assume the position of meditation. Assume the position of attention. Bow. Assume the position of repose.

This is the end of the black belt second kata.

All movements are in slow motion.

†Assume the position of repose facing east. Assume the position of attention. Assume the position of meditation. Assume a horse stance with your fists at your sides.

577

578

579

580

581

577. Extend your arms outward, palms down, as you slide your feet together.

578. In a circular movement, bring your extended arms forward.

579-581. There is no hesitation between the postures shown in these photos. The movement is continuous. Make a full circle movement with your extended arms and finish with your arms extended forward, as in photo 578.

582

583

584

585

586

587

582. Step to the side with your right foot as you place your arms forearm over forearm, your left arm on top, palms down.

583. Step to the northeast with your left foot and assume a slashing guard position with your left hand high and your right hand at chest height.

584. Draw your open right hand to your side, palm up, as you slash/block upward with your left hand.

585. Slash/block down and outward with your left hand.

†Assume the guard position as in photo 583.

| 588 | 589 | 590 |

586. Slash/block down with your right hand as you draw your left open hand to your side.

587. As you extend your left hand into a slashing guard position, draw your right elbow back.

588. Stab to the northeast with your right hand as you draw your open left hand to your side.

†Assume the slashing guard position as in photo 583.

589. Step to the southeast with your right foot and assume a slashing guard, leading with your right hand.

590. Slash/block upward with your right hand and draw your open left hand in front of your chest.

591. Slash/block downward with your right hand as you draw your left hand to your side.

591

592   593   594

592. Slash downward with your left hand as you draw your right open hand to your side.

593. Draw your left elbow back as you slash to the south with your right hand, then . . .

594. . . . stab to the southeast with your left hand as you draw your right hand to your side.

†Assume the guard position as in photo 589.

595. Step to the east with your left foot and assume a slashing guard leading with your left hand and draw your right hand to your side.

596. Parry outward with the back of your right hand as you draw your open left hand to your side.

597. Parry cross-body with your right hand.

†Draw your open right hand to your side as you resume the slashing guard position with your left hand as in photo 595.

598. Stab forward with your right hand as you draw your left hand to your side.

†Draw your right hand to your side and resume the slashing guard position as in photo 595.

599. Deliver a heel-of-palm blow upward with your right hand as you draw your left hand to your side.

600. Resume the guard position, leading with your left open hand as you draw your right hand to your side.

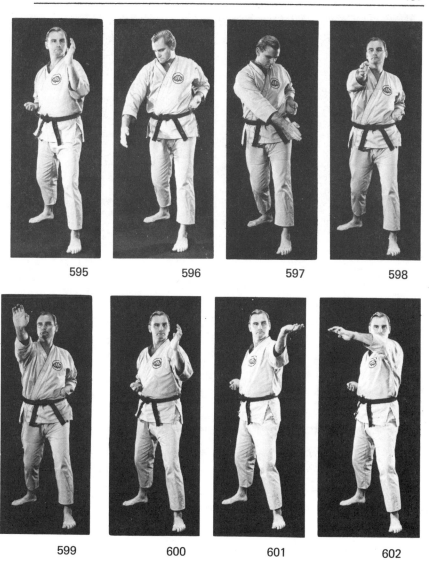

595   596   597   598

599   600   601   602

601. Deliver a high cross-body slash with your left hand, palm up.

602. Turn your hand over and deliver a high back-handed slash, palm down.

603   604   605

603. Step forward with your right foot and assume a
high slashing guard, leading with your right hand as you
draw your left hand to your side.

604. Parry to the north with the back of your left hand as
you draw your right hand to your side.

605. Parry cross-body with your left hand as you fist your
right hand.

†Assume the guard position as in photo 603.

606. As you draw your right hand to your side, stab forward
with your left hand.

†Resume the guard position as in photo 603.

607. As you draw your right hand to your side, deliver a high
heel-of-palm blow with your left hand.

†Resume the guard position as in photo 603.

608. Deliver a cross-body slash to the north with your right
hand, palm up.

609. Turn your hand palm down and slash to the south.

610. Step back with your right foot and raise your right
hand into a high slashing guard position, placing the back of
your left hand under your elbow.

606 607 608 609

610 611 612

611. Reverse the position. Step back with your left foot as you raise your left hand in a high slashing guard and place your right hand under your elbow.

612. Step back with your left foot and assume a horse stance with your fists at your sides.

†Assume the position of meditation. Assume the position of attention. Bow. Assume the position of repose.

This is the end of the black belt third kata.

613

614

615

616

BLACK BELT — FOURTH KATA

All movements are in slow motion.

†Assume the position of repose facing east. Bow. Assume the position of attention. Assume a horse stance with your fists at your sides.

613. Without moving your left foot, turn your right foot toward the south, look to the south, and place your right fist over your left fist.

614. Draw your right foot up to your left knee.

615. Kick to the south, using an edge-of-foot blow.

617

618

619

620

616. Recover with your right foot advanced toward the south. Make a back-knuckle blow with your right fist and place your left hand under your right elbow.

617. Without stepping, pivot on both feet, turning counter-clockwise to face north and bring your hands to your right side, fist-over-fist.

618. Draw your left foot to your right knee.

619. Kick to the north with an edge-of-foot blow.

620. Recover facing north with your left foot advanced. Make a back-knuckle blow with your left hand and place your right hand under your left elbow.

621 622 623 624

621. Step to the east with your right foot, look toward the east and draw your hands to your left side, fist-over-fist.

622. Draw your right foot to your left knee.

623. Kick to the east with an edge-of-foot blow.

624. Recover with your right foot advanced toward the east. Make a back-knuckle blow with your right hand and place your left hand under your right elbow.

625. Without stepping, pivot on both feet to look toward the west, your hands fist-over-fist at your right side.

†Draw your left foot to your right knee, and . . .

626. . . . deliver an edge-of-foot kick to the west.

627. Recover with your left foot advanced and strike down with your left fist.

628. Pivot on your left foot and turn counterclockwise as you deliver a roundhouse kick with your right foot and raise your left hand into a high guard; then, without lowering your right leg, swing slowly around counterclockwise to . . .

629. . . . face east and recover into a low fist guard leading with your right fist and right foot. Draw your left fist to your side.

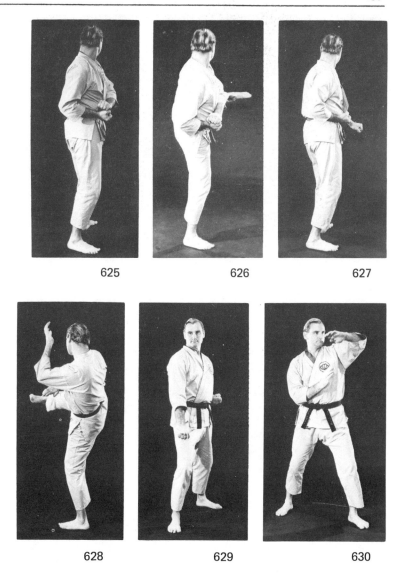

625 626 627

628 629 630

630. Step forward with your left foot and assume a slashing guard with your left hand high and your right hand at chest height.

631   632   633

631. Step with your right foot and assume a slashing guard with your right hand high.

632. Step to the east with your left foot and slash forward with your left hand as you draw your right hand to your side.

633. Turning clockwise, step around with your left foot, crossing it in front of your right foot. You have turned your body 180 degrees toward the west. Your left hand is in a high slashing guard, your right hand is at waist height, palm down.

634. As you bring your hands to your left side, fist-over-fist, pivot counterclockwise on your left foot and then deliver a circle kick with your right foot.

635, 636. Recover with your right leg crossed in front of your left leg. Shift your weight to your right foot and deliver a circle kick with your left foot.

637. Recover into a horse stance facing east.

634

635

636

637

†Assume the position of meditation. Assume the position of attention. Bow. Assume the position of repose.

This is the end of the black belt fourth kata.

638   639   640

BLACK BELT — FIFTH KATA

All movements are in slow motion.

†Start from the position of repose facing east. Bow. Assume the position of attention. Assume the position of meditation.

638. Step to the side with your right foot and assume a horse stance with your elbows close to your body and your forearms extended, fists up.

639. With a sweeping movement of your arms, slash/block up to the south with both hands.

†Assume the horse stance as in photo 638.

640. With a sweeping movement, slash/block upward to the north with both hands.

†Return to the horse stance as in photo 638. Your hands and arms remain in the extended-forearms position for the next six moves.

641. Draw your right foot to your left knee, then . . .

642. . . . kick to the south with an edge-of-foot blow.

643. Recover with your right foot crossed behind your left foot.

641

642

643

644

645

644. Shift your weight onto your right foot and draw your left foot to your right knee.

645. Deliver an edge-of-foot kick to the north.

646   647   648

649   650   651

646-648. Recover with your left foot crossed behind your right foot and start to pivot counterclockwise, putting your hands on the floor when you are facing west, and deliver a high, back stamping kick with your right foot.

649, 650. As you rise, pivot on your left foot and swing your right foot around, turning counterclockwise to assume the horse stance with your fists at your sides.

651. Step forward with your left foot and assume a cat stance with your weight on your right foot and the ball of your left foot resting lightly on the floor. Your knees are slightly bent. Assume a slashing guard with your left hand raised and your right hand palm up.

652

653

654

655

656

652. Draw your left foot to your right knee.

653. Deliver a stamping kick forward.

654. Recover with your left foot advanced. Deliver a high slash/block with your right hand as you draw your open left hand to your side.

655. Stab straight forward with your left hand as you draw your open right hand to your side.

656. Step forward with your right foot and assume a cat stance, with your right hand in a high slashing guard as you draw your open left hand to your side.

657

658

659

660

661

662

657. Draw your right foot to your left knee.

658. Deliver a stamping kick forward.

659. Recover with your right foot advanced. Block/slash high with your left hand as you draw your open right hand to your side.

660. Stab straight out with your right hand as you draw your open left hand to your side.

663   664   665

661. Pivot counterclockwise on both feet to face west with your left foot advanced. Your right hand is in a high slashing guard and your left hand is placed under your right elbow, palm down.

†Draw your left foot to your right knee, and . . .

662. . . . deliver a high stamping kick.

663. Recover with your left foot crossed in front of your right foot, your left hand in a high slashing guard and your right hand palm down under your left elbow.

664. Deliver a roundhouse kick with your right foot.

665. Recover with your right foot crossed in front of your left foot, your right hand in a high slashing guard and your left hand under your right elbow.

666. Draw your left foot to your right knee and deliver a stamping kick.

666

667   668   669

670   671

667. Recover with your left foot crossed in front of your right foot and look to the east. Your left hand is in a high slashing guard with your right hand under your elbow.

668. Shift your weight onto your left foot and draw your right foot to your left knee, and . . .

669-671. . . . kick with an edge-of-foot blow and recover into a horse stance with your fists at your sides. Return to the position of meditation.

†Assume the position of attention. Bow. Assume the position of repose. *This completes the black belt kata series.*

SPARRING

Sparring, or kumite, is the contest-like practice of karate. For some players it is the precursor to tournament karate play. For others, it is a way to play karate as an exercise and for recreation in conjunction with ongoing practice of the routines. Still other people enjoy sparring as the sole method of practice after having learned basic technique. The advantage of sparring is its flexibility and variety. No two karate sparring sessions are the same; the possible variations of combinations of techniques in offense and defense, and in counters, is virtually without limit.

While practice and performance of the kata and waza routines develops technique which can be refined by many repetitions, skill in kumite is developed in several ways. Players can work out favored combinations and refine them for planned offense play or by-chance use. They can develop responsive techniques for quick defense-and-counter reactions. They can learn to "read" a sparring partner's style in the first minute of play and then adopt a strategy to correspond to the specific opponent. All of these skills make for good and exciting karate sparring.

For independent study and for physical education I would suggest that players begin by practicing give-and-take sparring before engaging in free-style kumite.

CAUTION: In the practice and demonstration of katas and wazas, the full range of body targets is used, including old-style karate point areas. Because each of the partners has a strictly defined role in the formal routines, and they rehearse cooperatively, the possibility of accidental contact is slight. The situation is significantly different in sparring. A different set of rules should be followed to ensure safety in practice. For give-and-take and for free-style sparring, use the low-risk targets explained on page 205.

STANCES

In filmed karate fight scenes, the adversaries usually take an exotic-looking fighting stance before going into their act. The script and the situation allow the action to stop while the karate fighter holds his intimidating stance. Real life self-defense situations are not so accommodating. Stances are seldom practical for street defense.

672   673

The principal value of karate fighting stances is for tactical use in sparring and contest. The opponent players are not assaulting each other, but are moving about, looking for an opportunity to score a point.

The stance, or the choice of no stance, would depend on the strategy and tactics and individual preference of the players.

672. A "T" guard stance gives good, strong balance, allows flexibility of response, ease of movement in all directions and a quick shift to offensive play.

673. Leading with his right, the player takes a wider "T" foot position and with his lead hand extended further forward, he can block/guard and quickly advance for a point-scoring offense.

674. The cat stance, with weight shifted to the rear foot, is favored by some players for the ease with which kicks can be delivered. The disadvantage is the relative weakness of balance from front to back.

675. Here the player assumes a cat stance with his lead hand in a low guard.

676. This stylized one-point balance is seldom used in sparring. A highly skilled player might use it for an instant to precede a snap-kick point attempt, but would not hold it.

674   675

676   677

677. The horse stance with the side of the body presented to the opponent player is a strong-balance position, excellent for defense and appropriate for kicking offense. Some people find that the horse stance limits maneuvering; they feel too heavily braced to move lightly, quickly and responsively.

Stances should not be static. A good player will shift from stance to stance as he moves about looking for an opportunity to move in for scoring. Good sparring is active/responsive. An attack stance, readying for an attempt to score, will shift to a defense stance if the opponent player attempts a point-making technique.

Beginners tend to adopt a purely defensive or purely offensive stance, but this makes for dull play. In response to a static offensive stance, the opponent player is likely to adopt a static defensive posture; this would result in a stalemate.

The ability to move around, changing stances from high to low guards, from left-leading to right-leading positions, changing from strong defense to attack position, is developed with practice. With experience and experimentation you will discover the stances which are appropriate and comfortable for your individual style.

FEINTING

A feint, or fake, is a deliberately misleading tactic made to get a specific reaction from the opponent player.

Fakes and feints can be used to draw the opponent player out to reveal his style of defense, and to set him up for an attempt to score.

For example, a fake high blow can divert the opponent player into putting up a high guard, which leaves him open to a scoring blow into the upper thigh (low area). Or you can feint with a kick, to which your opponent responds with a low block, allowing you to deliver a high point-scoring hand blow.

Feinting also includes sudden moves to one side, getting a response to that side so that you can deliver your intended scoring tactic to the unprotected side. Random movements, such as boxers use, can also be utilized as feinting, distracting tactics.

PIVOT-AND-KICK

678-680. The pivot and kick is a technique and a tactic. It is a relatively difficult maneuver, but an excellent planned or by-chance move.

The left man attempts a forward kick which his opponent evades by drawing back. Using the momentum of his swinging leg, he spins around and delivers a backward kick toward the upper arm or upper chest.

678

679

680

681

TOKEN BLOCKING

In addition to standard block and parry actions, in which the blocking arm or hand make contact with the intended blow, token blocking is also used in sparring.

681-683. A token block is made by placing the hand or arm so that it is an obstacle to the intended blow. The open hand, the palm, the back of the hand, or the forearm can be used in token blocking to invalidate a point-scoring attempt.

GRAB & PULL

Grappling--holding on to an opponent to immobilize him-- is not included in karate sparring. But a player may grab cloth and pull the opponent forward to deliver a light-touch scoring point. When the point blow is delivered, the grip must be released immediately.

682

683

GIVE-AND-TAKE

Give-and-take is an interim practice procedure which gives players the experience of working in an unrehearsed manner and prepares them for the next step, which is free-style sparring.

Give-and-take is easier than sparring because players need only be concerned with offense or with defense. In free-style sparring, they must plan offensive play at the same time that they are actively defending against the opponent's attempts to score.

Give-and-take goes back and forth; one player takes the offensive role and then takes the defense.

When it is your turn to score, or attempt to score, your partner may use any defensive tactics, but may not attempt an offense or a counter. In the defensive role, the player is limited to blocks, parries, and evasive body and foot movements.

When you have practiced in give-and-take long enough to become familiar with the feeling of moving around as you make unrehearsed, flexible combinations of the basic techniques, then you can begin sparring free style.

NEW RULES FOR SPARRING

The targets for scoring points are the most vulnerable body areas--head, face and eyes, throat, midsection and kidneys. The choice of these target areas is a direct reflection of outmoded goals. Combat is confused with sport.

Traditionalists argue that authentic karate is karate played by the old rules. But fencing and archery, which also derive from combat skills, have been modified to meet the objectives of modern sport; the risk of injury has been reduced without diminishing the pleasure and the physical benefits.

Karate rules have been made by humans, not by gods. The rules are not immutable; they can be changed to protect the safety of the players.

Sparring can and should be oriented to the well-being, health and pleasure of the *participants.*

Technically, and according to the rules, contact blows are prohibited in most karate sport contest. In some tournaments, contact is allowed but the players wear protective gear and gloves.

In the no-contact play, by the traditional rules, points are awarded for blows delivered to within two inches of the intended target. That is, a point is gained if the defending player does not block, parry, or move out of the two-inch range.

Two problems arise from this situation: Point blows are not easy to judge. Accidental or deliberate contact may result in serious injury because of the vulnerable target areas.

HIGH-RISK/LOW-RISK TARGETS

By changing the point targets from high-risk-of-injury body areas to relatively low-risk-of-injury body areas, karate sparring can become an activity which is entirely consistent with the objectives of physical education--health, fitness and fun.

Instead of hitting toward the head, face, eyes, throat and midsection, the target can be changed to the upper chest, upper back, upper arm and upper thigh. The consequences of even a forceful accidental blow to these areas is significantly less serious than the consequences of a blow struck into the high-risk areas.

Highly skilled players can control their blows with great precision--most of the time. But most people playing karate are not highly skilled. New players have relatively little control. If a highly skilled player makes accidental contact into a high-risk body area, he is striking a vulnerable target with a dangerously forceful blow. Less skilled players are not so likely to strike with great force, but they are more likely to make contact when the reference point is thin air. For this reason, I have adopted the procedure of allowing *light contact* to *low-risk areas.* When light contact is made, both players can feel that a scoring point has been made. When contact is made to the low-risk areas, a less-than-perfectly-controlled blow is unlikely to be dangerous.

Changing the rules to light contact to low-risk targets does not diminish the skill required to score a point. Blocking or evading a touch to the upper chest is as difficult for the defending player and demonstrates as much skill in tactical offensive play. Changing the rules to light contact to low-risk targets does not diminish the skill required for karate sparring. It takes as much defensive skill to block a touch to the chest as it does to block a blow toward the eyes. It takes as much tactical offensive skill to complete a light touch to the upper arm as to hit into the head. Unopposed touch-kicking to the upper back is as difficult as kicking within two inches of the kidney area.

Using the traditional rules and targets for sparring and contest, this would be a good point-scoring blow in no-contact karate.

Distance is critical. This would not be close enough to earn a point. Here, the left man is shown stationary, but . . .

*. . . in actual sparring, as the right man is
making his point-scoring attempt . . .*

*. . . he could misjudge the distance and make
contact, or . . .*

. . . the left player might move in at the same
moment to attempt to score, thus putting
himself into contact with the hand blow.

When the face is the target area, contact
with a forceful blow is needlessly violent,
but if the scoring attempt is made with a
stab toward the eyes . . .

. . .extremely high risk of serious, permanent injury is involved.

The skill required to score point blows is the same when the targets are changed from high-risk to low-risk. Light-touch contact with a fingertip blow to the upper chest is a good test of proficiency.

*Equal defensive skill is required to block a
blow directed toward a low-risk or . . .*

. . . a high-risk target area.

An open hand slash toward the throat is high risk. The risk can be removed without reducing the benefits and pleasure of karate sparring. Instead of hitting toward the throat, use light-touch contact to the upper chest.

Instead of kicking toward the groin, the target can be changed to the upper thigh. Accidental contact to the groin is excrutiatingly painful. Equal skill would be required to score by light-touch contact to the upper thigh.

*The vulnerable kidney area is a target in
traditional karate. Kicking and . . .*

*. . . punching blows are used. Accidental
forceful contact could have serious and
permanent consequences.*

Back body targets can be changed to the low-risk upper back and . . .

. . . the low-risk upper arm.

Instead of kicking toward the head or face, . . .

*. . . a low-risk target could be used. Either
the upper arm or upper back.*

Blocking a high kick is much the same if a low-risk target is used.

CHALK SPARRING

Chalk sparring is a test of ability that can be done with equal pleasure by beginners and highly skilled players. The strategy and tactics of sparring can be practiced and developed, there is no risk of injury, and chalk sparring is fun to watch.

The procedure is simple. Each player holds a piece of chalk in each hand. The object is to mark the opponent player's uniform (or T-shirt) at the low-risk areas. They start from stances of their choice and then move about, as in standard sparring practice, but "hand blows" represented by chalk marks, are the only offensive tactics allowed. All of the defenses, blocking, parrying, and evading are permitted, and, of course, countering.

At the end of a specified time, the player with the fewer chalk marks is the "winner."

SPARRING PROCEDURE

Different procedures are followed for different forms of
sparring. If you are sparring for exercise and fun, you can
set your own pattern of play within the general guidelines.

If sparring is being evaluated by a teacher or committee (for
belt rank promotion) the procedures will be adapted by them
to suit the requirements of the school or club.

Players practicing kumite face each other at a distance out of
striking range. They bow to each other. They assume stances
of their choice and begin to move about within the designated
practice area and attempt to score points. In free play, no
one counts the score, as would be done in contest, but after
each successful score is made, the players back away from
each other and start again to move about in free-style kumite.

The length of time spent in sparring practice will depend on
the players. Beginners can start with two minutes of sparring
and increase to three minutes or longer as skill and endurance
are developed.

At the end of the sparring session, partners bow to each other
before leaving the practice area.

If sparring is for demonstration of skill, the candidates approach
the practice area and bow to the teacher in unison. If there
is more than one person evaluating the test, the candidates bow
to each of them. Then they face each other and bow. They
assume the stances of their choice and kumite for the time
allowed by the specific rules of the club or teacher.

Since sparring is contest-like, but is not contest, there is no
winner, even though points are counted.

If, for example, the teacher requires that candidates for
promotion must show point-winning ability in sparring by
scoring twice in two three-minute periods, it is possible that
both candidates could fulfill that requirement. As in practice
sparring, the players back away from each other after a
point-scoring technique. At a signal from the judge or teacher,
they continue to spar, unless it is indicated that the time has
elapsed. At the end of each sparring period, the players bow
to each other and to the tteacher or judges before leaving the
area.

CREATIVE KARATE

If you become interested in ongoing karate practice and do not have access to formal instruction, or you do not have a practice partner with whom to spar or you do not enjoy the sparring aspects of karate, there is another, creative approach you can take--invention!

When you have completed the study and practice of all the katas, if you are working alone, develop new combinations of techniques you have learned and put together your own kata routines. There is no limit to the amount of time and effort you can put into this activity and there is no limit to the number of different routines you could create for your own pleasure and recreation.

If you are working with a partner, you could combine your creative efforts to develop new kata routines and new waza routines.

There is a tremendous sense of accomplishment when you can learn and perform the prearranged routines with style and grace. There is even greater pleasure in going beyond the constrictions of already choreographed series of movements to express yourself through creative movement.

CHOOSING A SCHOOL

Many people who are introduced to karate through reading become interested in supervised instruction. And the most common inquiry from readers is: "How can I choose a school or teacher?"

If you live in a community which has a school, observe a class in session and then you can decide whether or not the teacher suits you. If there is more than one school, visit them and compare. You are the best judge of what is appropriate for you even though you do not have a technical background. You are equipped with a more important gauge for making a decision--your own reaction to what you see!

Any reliable school or teacher will allow you to observe at least one complete session before you make up your mind. Verbal explanations of what is being taught are not enough; you have to see what it is. Nor should you allow yourself to be dazzled by what the teacher can do. You are not paying to see him perform; you are paying him for what he can teach *you* to do.

When you observe a class, watch the teacher and watch the students. Does the teacher actually instruct? Does he give clear directions and explain what is to be done, or does he merely demonstrate and leave the students to imitate as well as they can? Is the teacher patient and does he encourage the students, or is he cross and rude to students who need correction or help?

Do the students seem enthusiastic about what they are doing? Do they appear to be helpful to one another? Is there a friendly atmosphere?

Is the material being practiced what you think *you* would like to learn?

If you like what you see, the school is right for you. If you don't like what you see, the school is not right for you, even though the teacher, the material and the method might be quite acceptable to other individuals.

DON'T SIGN A CONTRACT unless you are absolutely certain that you understand what you are signing and that it is a fair contract. Unless you are familiar with contracts, you may need help in deciding whether or not the contract protects your consumer rights. If you sign a contract without reading or understanding it, you may find yourself obligated to pay for lessons you don't want to take or you may find that you cannot get a refund in case of emergency.

As a general rule, you are better protected if you make partial payments as you go along than if you pay for a full course in advance. If you make partial payments and then change your mind or lose interest or move, you are not tied to an arrangement which might be a financial burden.

If you need help in deciding if a contract is fair, if a financial arrangement is fair, or if the operator of a school is reliable, ask your local Chamber of Commerce or your librarian to direct you. Most communities have agencies which offer free advice and guidance in these matters.

It is your money and your time which are being spent. You have the right to spend them the way you please and to make sure that you will get your money's worth.

INDEX

BRUCE TEGNER was born in Chicago, Illinois in 1929. Both of his parents were professional teachers of judo and jujitsu; they began his formal instruction in the martial arts when Bruce was two years old!

In a field in which most individuals concentrate on a narrow specialty, Bruce Tegner's experience was unusual. His education covered many aspects of weaponless fighting of many styles, as well as sword and stick techniques. At the age of twenty-one, after becoming California state judo champion, he gave up competition to devote himself to research, course development, teaching, and teacher-training.

In the U.S. armed forces Mr. Tegner trained instructors to teach unarmed combat; he taught military police tactics; he coached sport judo teams. Later, he trained actors and devised and choreographed fight scenes for movies and television. From 1952 through 1957 he operated his own school in Hollywood California, where he taught men, women, and children, exceptionally gifted students, and blind and disabled persons. With his colleague and sometimes co-author, Alice McGrath, he developed many special courses and teaching methods, some of which have been adopted by physical education departments, martial arts schools, and police academies throughout the world.

Bruce Tegner books range from basic, practical self-defense to exotic forms of fighting for experts and enthusiasts. Editions of Tegner books have been published in German, Spanish, Portuguese, Dutch, and French.

BRUCE TEGNER books are on sale at bookstores throughout the world. If your local dealer does not stock the titles you want, you may order directly from the publisher.

FOR A FREE brochure describing the complete line of Bruce Tegner books on self-defense, judo, karate, kung fu, tai chi and other specialties in this field, and a listing of the inspirational books of *ELLEN KEI HUA* , write to:

Thor Pub Co.
P O Box 1782
Ventura CA 93002